# ROWBOTHAM

QUARTERMAN (I)

2

# Rowbotham

## Rev. A. Huckett

© A. Huckett 2002
Published by the World Ship Society, Gravesend, Kent DA12 5UB
ISBN 0 905617 97 5

Cover: CHEVIOT painting by A.K. Branden          Andrew Huckett Collection

# CONTENTS

WHEELSMAN (II) Andrew Huckett Collection

# INTRODUCTION AND ACKNOWLEDGEMENTS

Interest in Rowbotham Tankships Ltd. developed during my time as chaplain to The Missions to Seamen in Milford Haven in the second half of the 1980s. Hardly a day went by without at least one Rowbotham ship being in the Haven, either alongside at one of the oil terminals, at anchor in Dale Roads, or undergoing repairs in Milford Docks. During my five and a half years in Milford Haven I visited every member of the then current Rowbotham fleet. Talking on board to officers and crew, especially those who had served the company for a long time, I realised that there was a story to tell. I began to compile a fleet list which then led on to research into the company history. I was fortunate in my regular contacts with Captain John Phillips, at that time Rowbotham's Manager and Marine Superintendent in Milford Haven, who supplied me with information as well as put me in touch with various people who greatly assisted my researches.

One was Mr Richard ("Dick") Rowbotham, grandson of the founder of the company, Christopher Rowbotham. In the 1960s he had undertaken his own research into his family and had written a short history of the company which was published in the Rowbotham Group's house journal. I am grateful for his permission to use the fruits of his research, particularly concerning the family, and to quote parts of his history.

At the time that I commenced my researches the late Mr Albert Shaw was Managing Director of Rowbotham Tankships Ltd. I am most grateful for his encouragement and assistance in seeking out what little archive material remained after the company's records were destroyed in 1940, and for having the paintings of the company's earliest ships, which were displayed in the Boardroom, photographed. Thanks are also due to his successor, Mr Nick Josephy, for answering several questions concerning the company's later history.

Two long-serving, and now retired, directors of the company were very helpful in providing information concerning the history of the company and its ships, and in answering my various questions. Mr Edward Tombs provided corrections and additional information to my original draft and enlightened me on the mysteries of "Contracts of Affreighments". Mr Keith Barnett read and commented on a later draft and provided useful information, particularly on technical matters relating to the ships.

My thanks are extended to Dr Charles Waine for reading a draft copy of the history and for providing me with a copy of freight rates taken from Christopher Rowbotham's note book now in the possession of Mr Richard Rowbotham. To Mr William Schell for information on the Y-Tankers and other American-owned wartime vessels. (The source for the fact that Rowbotham managed some "Y-Tankers" came from documents held at the Public Record Office.) To Mr R. Hackman for supplying launch dates. To Stephen Rabson, P&O Librarian, for information concerning the period when the company was P&O owned. And to Ken Garrett for reading and commenting on the document.

Letters to Marine News, Ships Monthly, Sea Breezes and Shipping Today and Yesterday produced a number of responses. My thanks, in particular, to Captain F.J. Gilbert, Captain John Harvey, the late Mr Robert Sutherland and Mr John Bellaby, all of whose reminiscences I have included in the text or, in the case of the latter three, as appendices. Thanks are also due for their contributions to Captain C.L. Reynolds, Messrs D. Butler (Odfjell Tankers (S) Pte. Ltd.), J. Chapman, A.M. Connell (Richard Dunston (Hessle) Ltd.), R. Griffin, S.

Meech (Texaco), G. Mobbs and B. Payne.

No WSS publication would be possible without the efforts of members of the Publication Committee, Central Record and World Ship Photo Library. I am very grateful to Roy Fenton and Harold Appleyard for their guidance and advice in the preparation of this history. Thanks are also extended to the members of Central Record who checked the fleet list, Mr A. Hague, Mr J.L. Loughran (Ships' Liveries), Mr Cliff Parsons (Negative Library) and Mr R.A. Smith (Print Library).

All photographs are acknowledged and come from a variety of sources. Thanks are extended to all who provided photographs and for their correspondence. To Lord Greenway, Dr D. Jenkins (Welsh Industrial and Maritime Museum) and Messrs. G.R. Atkinson, J.K. Byass, B.F. Bridges, N.I. Cutts, D.Davies, W.E.D. Docker, D. Hocquard, T. Holmes, J.W.Kennedy, B. & D. McCall and Wm. A. Schell.

Research was carried out at Lloyd's Register, where I received valuable assistance from Barbara Jones and Anne Cowne; the National Maritime Museum, Greenwich; the Public Record Office, Kew; the Guildhall Library and the Imperial War Museum.

Sources consulted have included the following:

Lloyd's Register.
Lloyd's Confidential Register.
Lloyd's Weekly Casualty Reports.
Lloyd's List.
Ministry of War Transport papers and ships' registers held at the Public Record Office.
Service List for First World War (Ministry of Shipping).
Service Lists for Second World War.
'Empire Ships of World War II' by W.H. Mitchell & L.A. Sawyer.
'Sailing Ship to Supertanker' by W.H. Mitchell & L.A. Sawyer.
'Empire Tugs' by W.J. Harvey & K. Turrell.
'Cory Towage Ltd' by W.J. Harvey.
'Everard of Greenhithe' by K.S. Garrett.
'Steam Coasters and Short Sea Traders' by Charles V. Waine.
'A Sideways Launch' (History of James Pollock, Sons & Co. Ltd.) by Anne Salmon.
'The Anglo-Saxon/Shell Tankers' by N.L. Middlemiss.
'An Experience Shared 1939-1945' by Vernon Scott.
'US Army Ships and Watercraft of World War II' by David Grover.
Articles in 'Tees Packet' (Journal of the Teesside Branch of the WSS) by James Layton.

This history and fleet list is dedicated to all sea and shore staff who served with Rowbotham over the years.

Andrew W. Huckett
27 The Finches
Sittingbourne
Kent ME10 4PY

# THE HISTORY OF THE COMPANY

The development of the internal combustion engine, and thus the motor car, was directly responsible for the introduction of the coastal tanker. With the increased popularity of the motor car there was a demand for a widespread distribution of petroleum to all parts of the country to fuel this new mode of transport. Initially distribution was undertaken by rail from the tank farms, established by the various oil companies near to major ports, to where the refined products were brought by ocean going tankers from refineries in the oil producing countries. With the increase in demand for petroleum it soon became economical to use small coastal tankers to supply the smaller ports around the UK coast.

One of the first shipping companies to be attracted to this new trade was the firm of C. Rowbotham & Sons of London. The name Rowbotham was to become synonymous with the carriage of clean, that is refined, petroleum products. The company was also to become the owner of one of Britain's largest coastal tanker fleets.

C. Rowbotham & Sons was a family firm whose origins went back to one Christopher Rowbotham, a native of Knottingley in Yorkshire. Born in 1851, Christopher Rowbotham was one of a family of at least eight children. In the parish records his father's occupation was given as "haulier". This was a man who hauled boats along the canals and rivers which abounded in that part of Yorkshire. From research undertaken by Mr Richard ("Dick") Rowbotham, the grandson of Christopher Rowbotham, we know that his father died when Christopher was only seven years old.

In 1863 Christopher's mother married again. It is believed that shortly afterwards, because of a quarrel with his step-father, he ran away to sea. Nothing is known of Christopher's early life at sea but, in 1872, he is recorded as being master of the schooner TIGER of Goole. He was only twenty. As Dick Rowbotham wrote in his history of the Rowbotham Group: "As he appears on the articles of his previous ship, the RESOLUTE of Goole, as steward, his promotion was fairly rapid by any standards and it is interesting to note that his pay as steward was £1.9.0 per month. He remained master of the TIGER until 1874 when he became master of the schooner ARRIVAL of London, owned by a Robert Cawthorn of Knottingley, who was a relative of the family. He was master of the ARRIVAL for five years."

The RESOLUTE was an iron screw three mast schooner-rigged vessel of 240g, while the two vessels of which Christopher Rowbotham was master were somewhat smaller. The TIGER, of 65g, was built at Wakefield in 1864 for Thomas Clegg of Goole. ARRIVAL was slightly larger at 77g, and was built in 1869 by Atkinson of Knottingley. Christopher signed on as her master on 3rd February, 1874, and remained with her until April 1879. As well as achieving the position of master at an early age, Christopher also married while still relatively young. He was still a minor of 19 when he married Ann Andrews, daughter of a wealthy Liverpool ship rigger, in Goole in 1871.

## First steps in shipowning

The year 1879 was a watershed in the career of Christopher Rowbotham, for in that year he entered the world of shipowning, albeit as a partner. The vessel concerned was the 100g wooden ketch PRINCESS which was completed in April 1879 by William Wake of Goole. Lloyd's Register records ownership being in the hands of G.J. King & Co. However, her certificate of registration records her actual owners as being:

Christopher Rowbotham of Goole, Master Mariner, 22 shares.
George James King of Goole, Master Mariner, 21 shares.
William Andrews of Liverpool, Rigger, 21 shares.

William Andrews was Christopher's father-in-law. By 1898 all shares had passed into the hands of Christopher Rowbotham. He was also PRINCESS' first master, a position he retained until 1885. As well as being the first vessel in the fleet PRINCESS became the last sailing vessel owned by the company, disposed of in 1917 after serving Rowbotham for nearly 38 years.

1885 was another important year for Christopher Rowbotham. In this year he relinquished command of PRINCESS, acquired a majority interest in the wooden schooner ATHLETAE and settled in Portsmouth. Here he began to develop a business in the movement of Admiralty stores which became the company's principal trade for many years, together with involvement in the coastal tramp trade. However, he did not remain in Portsmouth for long as, later the same year, he moved to London and took over the shipbroking business of a Mr T. Saunders, of 66 Lower Thames Street, whom he retained as cashier. In 1889 Christopher Rowbotham moved his office to 6 Water Lane, also in the City of London.

Four years after the acquisition of ATHLETAE a third vessel was added to the fleet. She was the 165g wooden schooner THUSNELDA which was renamed ELSIE after Christopher Rowbotham's eldest daughter who had been born in 1873. In 1890, following the loss of ATHLETAE, the 115g wooden schooner CELESTINA was purchased from Timothy White of Portsmouth. Both vessels did not long survive the advent of steam cargo ships into the fleet.

In 1899 Christopher Rowbotham acquired his first steam ship, the 258g CHEVIOT. She was followed, in 1903, by the 458g HELMSMAN (I), probably ordered as a result of an increase in Admiralty work due to the war in South Africa. This, the first steamer to be directly ordered by Christopher Rowbotham, also started the naming policy by which the company's ships have been distinguished ever since.

There was one exception. This was the 358g ARRIVAL, built in 1904, named after the vessel of which Christopher Rowbotham was master from 1874 to 1879. With three steamers in the fleet the sailing vessels CELESTINA and ELSIE were sold in 1904 and 1905 respectively.

By 1905, according to Dick Rowbotham, the office "staff consisted of six persons - the "old man", two sons William and Farnill, Saunders the cashier, Mathias the chartering clerk and "Timmo" (Percy Timms) as office boy." Percy Timms, working as a broker, went on to hold a directorship with the dry cargo chartering company. He completed 50 years with the company.

## C. Rowbotham & Sons

On 1st February, 1908, Christopher Rowbotham took his two sons, William and Farnill, into partnership with the establishment of the company as C. Rowbotham & Sons. The company also moved into new offices at 19 St. Dunstan's Hill from where they operated until the building was destroyed during the blitz in 1940.

In reply to a circular letter, dated 28th January 1908, advising the establishment of the partnership, George Elsmie & Son of 54 Market Street,

8

ARRIVAL                                    Andrew Huckett Collection

Aberdeen, owners of the North Eastern Shipping Co. Ltd., commented on changes in the shipping industry which had been experienced during the time they had been acquainted with Christopher Rowbotham. They wrote:

"There are great changes in the shipping world since we knew him first, both in the rates of freight and in the mode of carrying. Then it was all sailing craft. This firm had at one time as high as 10/- for granite setts from Aberdeen to London, and now, as you are aware, it is hardly possible to get more than 4/6, and in many instances a less rate than that is accepted. The sailing ship has practically disappeared, and there is now hardly anything else going but the steamer, and everything so keenly cut that unless you are fortunate in regard to weather conditions etc., and have everything ready at both ends, you would hardly pay expenses. If the law of progress is still to go on, what will it be 30 or 40 years after this!"

Considerable changes had taken place in the shipping industry during the previous thirty years. The steam ship had taken over from sail as the more efficient means of moving people and freight and as a result, together with the fall in shipbuilding costs, freight rates had fallen enormously. This even applied on the coastal trade where steam coasters, replacing the merchant schooner, were able to offer a quicker and reliable service, not so subject to weather and tidal conditions. For many owners the steam coaster was a sound economic proposition. Christopher Rowbotham followed the way of many other coastal shipping owners and, by 1909, the company were mainly operating steamers, the fourth, the 562g STEERSMAN (I), joining the fleet in that year.

Having reached the bottom of the slump freight rates began to rise from about 1910 with the build up in preparations for the First World War. More Admiralty stores were also being moved with the building of the Dreadnought battleships well in hand, as well as other elements of the Fleet.

# Admiralty business

A record of cargo freights for the period reveals something of the extent of Rowbotham's business with the Admiralty. For instance, in 1904 the sum of £95 is quoted for conveying one 6" gun and 10 tons of stores from Woolwich to Ullapool, while in February 1905 a quote of £60 is recorded for taking a 41' 10" steam pinnace from Portsmouth to the Tyne for the Naval Stores Officer, Portsmouth. The following month 6 masts, between 78 and 96 foot in length, were to be taken from Portsmouth to Pembroke Dock for the cost of £51.10.0. In May 1906 PRINCESS loaded 58 tons of filled shells at Upnor, on the river Medway, for Selby at 10/- per ton. As well as conveying guns, munitions, general stores, boilers and assorted boats, Rowbotham provided a quote for target towing.

"Secretary War Office re Target towing. ARRIVAL or CHEVIOT, 1 day not exceeding 10 hours commencing 7am £17 per day and £15 per day 8/- per hour extra, for 6 hours night work commencing 8pm. For one continuous week, Sunday excepted, average working 60 hours £95 and £90 - 8/- per hour extra. For one month, Sunday excepted, average working 60 hours weekly £90 and £85 per week."

On 24th August, 1906, a quote was sent to the Naval Ordinance Officer at Woolwich. "30/- per ton for not less than 60 tons guns, 15 tons each, for HMS COCHRANE Govan [COCHRANE was an armoured cruiser being built by Fairfield Shipbuilding & Engineering Co. Ltd., Govan], also £1 per ton for about 49 tons submarine mines and 2 tons ordinance Greenock/Woolwich." The quote being accepted the work was carried out by ARRIVAL.

All Royal Dockyards were visited by Rowbotham ships, as were many naval bases and shipbuilding yards constructing ships for the Royal Navy. In February 1906 boats were taken from Chatham to Barrow in Furness for the battleship HMS AFRICA at a cost of £122.10. In June 1907 ARRIVAL conveyed a 42' steam pinnace and 3 tons of gear from Portsmouth to Ellerman Lines' ADALIA (3847g/1899) in Millwall Docks for £37.10.0. In January 1911 a 10 ton small gun was taken from Woolwich to Hebburn, on the Tyne, for 15/- a ton. In March 250 tons of Oregon timber went from Chatham to Portsmouth at 6/9 a ton, while 124 tons went to Devonport for 7/- a ton. In September 1912 STEERSMAN carried 91 tons of loose boiler tubes between Devonport and Portsmouth at 6/- a ton, the voyage incurring a delay resulting in payment of 2 days demurrage.

# Diversification

On 17th August, 1911, Christopher Rowbotham, the founder of the company, died at his home at the age of 60.

Two years later, in 1913, the company diversified into the business of insurance with the transformation of the Insurance Department into a separate company, C. Rowbotham & Sons (Insurance) Ltd. This move towards diversification probably started when Christopher Rowbotham was elected to Lloyd's in 1909.

During the First World War, C. Rowbotham & Sons managed, or acted as agents for, a number of hopper barges on Government service. This is according to information extracted from the Ministry of Shipping's Service List, published in 1921. Barges LORD DEVONPORT, LORD POPLAR, LORD RITCHIE and LORD TILBURY were used at various times between 1916 and

1920 for carrying supplies for the Expeditionary Force between London and France, while LORD NORTHFLEET was based at Rochester. The floating derrick LORD PURFLEET was based on the Thames.

On behalf of the Admiralty, Rowbotham managed a total of 35 'X' class motor lighters. These carried a variety of military stores, plus coal, canteen stores, road material, fuel wood and shingle, mostly between London and France, but also from the Channel ports of Dover and Folkestone. One of these lighters, X57, J.J. Prior's converted coaster J.J. PRIOR, is thought to still be afloat as a floating home in London's docklands.

The Service List records that Rowbotham managed the paddle steamer SAINT TUDNO for a short period, taking over as managers in May 1918. They also acted as agents for the steam tug RECTOR which operated as a military tug based at Dunkirk.

Of its owned fleet the war years saw the HELMSMAN (I) employed as an ammunition carrier, while the oldest member of the fleet, PRINCESS, was sold in 1917, to be followed by CHEVIOT and ARRIVAL. The latter two were sold to take advantage of the high price for tonnage which the conflict had generated. This left Rowbotham with only two ships, HELMSMAN (I) and STEERSMAN (I).

In 1919 the company took on the management of two tugs on behalf of The Shipping Controller. These were the 419g tugs ST. TEATH and ST. TUDY. By the end of 1921 the vessels had been "taken out of our hand." This brief incursion into tugs was to hold the company in good stead when they returned to management on a larger scale during the Second World War.

1922 saw the company's next acquisition with the purchase of the 1394g WHEELSMAN (I). This was by far the largest vessel owned by the company to date. However, in the following year HELMSMAN (I) was sold out of the fleet, to be followed in 1925 by STEERSMAN (I), thus leaving WHEELSMAN (I) as the sole owned vessel.

This run down of the fleet was probably due to the termination of its contract to transport Admiralty stores at the end of 1924. In a letter dated 5th May the Director of Navy Contracts, in reference to "the coastwise freight of Government stores between Deptford Dockyard and various other Naval Establishments", informed the company:

"that as the Admiralty is now in a position to provide the necessary freight between these points in its own craft, there will be no further need to utilise the services of your vessels, and it is therefore necessary to give you requisite formal notice to terminate the contract."

The letter continues:

"the Department desires to take the opportunity of expressing its appreciation of the efficient and trustworthy manner in which, for nearly thirty years past, your firm has performed these services, and at all times filled their engagements with the Admiralty."

## Into the tanker trades

This loss of trade must have made Rowbotham seriously reconsider its position and led it ultimately to enter what was an entirely new area of activity, that of the carriage of petroleum products. It began with the acquisition, in

1925, of the 242g LOCHSIDE which had been used by her previous owners, James Deuchar, to convey beer from the Lochside brewery between Montrose and the Tyne, sometimes loading coal as a return cargo. She became the second HELMSMAN. She was sent to the yard of Clelands Graving Dock & Slipway Co. Ltd., at Wallsend on the river Tyne, where she was converted into an oil tanker by fitting tanks into her hold. Unfortunately, she was only to last two years in her new role as she was presumed to have foundered in a storm with the loss of all hands while on a voyage between the Medway and Stockton-on-Tees in 1927.

In 1925 William's son, Christopher, joined the company. He was to have an influential effect on the running of the company until its disposal in 1970. Farnill's son, John, joined the company in 1931.

Rowbotham re-entered the oil trade in 1928 when they bought the 1902-built CLYDEBURN, renamed her STEERSMAN (II) and converted her into an oil tanker by the insertion of portable tanks into her holds. She served as such for eight years before being broken up in 1936.

STEERSMAN (II)                                                        WSS

The Thirties were a time of deep depression which saw many shipping companies fail. In a farsighted move C. Rowbotham & Sons recognised the potential of their new area of activity for they placed an order with a Dutch shipyard for a new oil tanker. Delivered in October 1931 the TILLERMAN (I) achieved three firsts for the company. She was their first purpose built tanker, their first motor ship, and the first to be fitted with screw displace-ment pumps for cargo discharge. These were driven off a generator and auxiliary, supplied on a "no performance - no pay basis." One of TILLERMAN'S (I) first charterers was Russian Oil Products Ltd. (ROP). In November 1933 Rowbotham signed their first contract with Trinidad Leaseholds Ltd., with TILLERMAN (I) commencing to trade to Exeter City Basin for their account, traversing the Exeter Canal en route.

In March 1947 Trinidad Leaseholds Ltd. (TLL), formed in 1913, and the Texas Oil Co., formed in 1916 as the Texaco Petroleum Products Co. Ltd. but renamed in 1928, agreed to jointly market their petroleum products in the UK

TILLERMAN (I)                                    Andrew Huckett Collection

under the name of Regent Oil Co. Ltd., which became effective on 1st April 1948. Later in 1947 Caltex (California Texas Corporation), a joint venture formed in 1936 by the Standard Oil Co. of California and the Texaco Oil Co., bought the Texas Oil Co. and became joint owners of Regent Oil Co. Ltd. with Trinidad Leaseholds Ltd. In November of the following year Regent acquired Russian Oil Products Ltd. When Caltex terminated this joint marketing arrangement in the UK in 1967 Texaco Inc. took over full ownership of Regent Oil Co. Ltd. and changed its name to Texaco Ltd. In 1983 Rowbotham celebrated 50 years continuous contractual trading with Texaco and its predecessors TLL and ROP.

In 1934 a second tanker, the 360dwt RUDDERMAN (I), was delivered by the same Dutch builders who supplied TILLERMAN (I). Re-engined in 1958 she served the company until 1967 when, following an explosion she was sold for breaking up. On 27th May she had arrived at 8.55am from Douglas, Isle of Man, at the Ince coaster berth, on the Manchester Ship Canal, and was taking bunkers, having first de-ballasted, prior to loading at Stanlow. At approximately 10.50am an explosion occurred in her No. 3 starboard cargo tank, blowing the deck off and causing heavy damage to shell plating, bulkheads and deck fittings. There were no casualties.

1935 saw the end of the dry cargo side of the company when WHEELSMAN (I) was sold out of service. Latterly she had been engaged in carrying Blue Circle cement between the Medway and the Mersey.

Down again to two ships, but this time tankers, the company began an expansion which saw three new vessels added to the fleet prior to the beginning of the second world war. All came from the same Dutch yard which had built the company's first two purpose built tankers. The new vessels were the 355d WHEELSMAN (II), the 414d STEERSMAN (III) and the 271d GUIDESMAN (I). GUIDESMAN (I) was built especially for traversing the Exeter Canal which she continued to do until the trade ceased in 1964. All three ships served the company well into the 1960s.

Captain F.J. Gilbert, master of TILLERMAN (I) and then GUIDESMAN (I) for a total of eighteen months, from September 1952, describes the trade between

13

the Thames and Exeter. "These two small vessels kept the Exeter Regent depot supplied, the GUIDESMAN (I) being the largest vessel ever to run to Exeter, but the run was very hard in many of the prevailing westerly and south-westerly gales. Apart from that, it was very interesting, especially when negotiating the Exeter Canal. It could be quite an effort getting vessels up the canal in strong winds or during the summer months when water levels were very low, and certainly taught you a lot about shiphandling."

In 1938 C. Rowbotham & Sons returned to the field of tug management. On behalf of the Overseas Towage & Salvage Co. Ltd., a subsidiary of the French Compagnie de Remorquage et de Sauvetage "Les Abeilles", Rowbotham became managers of the 798g salvage tug NEPTUNIA. The company's towage base was established at Milford Haven. NEPTUNIA became the company's first casualty of the war when, on 13th September, 1939, she was sunk by the German submarine U-29 after leaving Falmouth to carry out salvage work in the North Atlantic. In all Rowbotham managed five tugs for Overseas Towage. The second was the slightly smaller SALVONIA, which remained under Rowbotham management until 1940, while the 327g NEREIDIA passed quickly to the French parent company. The other two were American tugs, SABINE and SEA GIANT, which were under management for the period of their delivery voyage from the United States to the UK.

## Rowbotham during the Second World War

All five of Rowbotham's own ships survived the war, serving as either tankers or water carriers in Government service or operating on behalf of the Petroleum Board. For instance, RUDDERMAN (I) was taken over by the Admiralty and acted as a water carrier in Icelandic waters for ships on Atlantic and Russian convoys, eventually being towed home. TILLERMAN (I) for a time was operating at Loch Ewe while STEERSMAN (III) operated under Admiralty contract taking fuel to the fleet at Scapa Flow. In 1944 RUDDERMAN (I), WHEELSMAN (II) and STEERSMAN (III) were attached to the Petroleum Board, while GUIDESMAN (I) was employed by the Admiralty on the Clyde.

The Petroleum Board had been formed in 1938 as a voluntary body by the major oil companies (Anglo-American Oil Co. Ltd., National Benzole Co. Ltd., Shell-Mex and B.P. Ltd., and Trinidad Leaseholds Ltd.) to act as a co-ordinating pool to control the importation, storage and distribution of oil products in the event of hostilities. Later the original pool was joined by thirty-two independent oil companies. With the declaration of war, under a Statutory Order, the Petroleum Board was given the monopoly to handle the distribution of all oil supplies within the country, whether for civilian or service use. Initially taking over twenty-one sea-going coastal tankers, with a total capacity of 10,000 tons, plus twelve vessels on time charter, during the war the number of vessels operated by the Board varied considerably depending on operational requirements. Early in 1944 the Board took over a large number of tankers in preparation for D-Day, increasing its capacity to 51,000 tons. By the end of 1944 tankers controlled by the Petroleum Board had carried six million tons of oil in the course of the war.

After the destruction of Rowbotham's office in St. Dunstans Hill in the blitz of 1940, together with all the company's records, the staff were initially evacuated to the country. They were set up in a barn in the grounds of White Gates at Sonning, the home of William C. Rowbotham, son of the founder and father of Christopher Rowbotham. The interior was converted to resemble an office.

RUDDERMAN (I)                                    Andrew Huckett Collection

Following their loss Captain "Dougie" Cable, the principal of Bulk Oil
Steamship Co. Ltd., offered Rowbotham the use of several rooms within
their offices at 130 Minories. The administrative staff moved into these
premises while the accounts continued to operate at Sonning until after the
war. In 1947 the company moved into re-furbished offices next door at
136-8 Minories. There the company remained until 1971.

Between 1940 and 1946 the company managed a total of twenty-five coastal
tankers, one ocean tanker, one dry cargo coaster and sixteen tugs on behalf
of the Ministry of Shipping, which in 1941 became the Ministry of War
Transport (MoWT). A number of the vessels were only under Rowbotham's
management for relatively short periods of time and, in fact, might have
been managed by several different companies during their wartime career.
Management changed depending on the employment of the vessel.

One area of employment was the management of all small service boats,
water carriers and harbour tugs at the Naval bases at Scapa Flow and the
Kyle of Lochalsh. One of the duties undertaken was the handling of most of
the mines that went through Scapa Flow. This involved transporting them
out to vessels standing off in the Roads.

Sixteen of the managed coastal tankers were part of the MoWT's
programme of war-time buildings. They consisted of several classes of
vessel. One came from the "Isles" class of 300d tankers (EMPIRE
ANGLESEY), while three were slightly smaller vessels but still of 300d
(EMPIRE GARNET/LAD, EMPIRE HOMESTEAD and EMPIRE NICKLEBY). Two
were 400d vessels (EMPIRE BARKIS and EMPIRE BOXER). The second most
numerous type built were the tankers of the "Empire Cadet" class.
Rowbotham managed five of these 800d vessels (EMPIRE ARTHUR, EMPIRE
DAMSEL, EMPIRE GYPSY, EMPIRE LASS and EMPIRE ORKNEY).

Numerically the largest class of coastal tanker built for the MoWT were the
43 vessels of the "Chant" class of 400d. These were built especially for the
Normandy invasion and the supply of forces in northern France.
Rowbotham managed five of these vessels (CHANTS 11, 12, 23, 25 and 27).
Two others were allocated to Rowbotham management, but in the event
were completed as general cargo coasters. These were to have been CHANT
29, which became EMPIRE FACTOR under the management of Ellerman
Wilson Line Ltd., and CHANT 31, which became EMPIRE FABLE under the
management of Robert Rix & Sons.

15

In 1944 Rowbotham took over six 1600d coastal tankers of the T1-M-A1 type which were bareboat chartered to the MoWT by the United States War Shipping Administration. They also became managers for nine of the United States Army's 1500d "Y" tankers which, like the "Chants", were built specifically for the supply of the Normandy beaches. Two (Y22 and Y23) were to be "allocated to the Armies of the Allies" for the D-Day operation, while seven (Y31, Y32, Y40, Y78, Y82, Y83 and Y107) were reported, in a document dated 22.12.1944, to have taken part in Operation Overlord under Rowbotham management. However, it is not clear whether the management was purely for technical matters or whether the company actually manned the vessels.

Rowbotham's only major casualty of the war, in addition to the tug NEPTUNIA, was their managed ocean tanker. After only one month in commission, on 24th August, 1944, the 2370d "Empire Pym" class EMPIRE ROSEBERY sunk after hitting a mine off the Normandy beaches at Arromanches. Vernon Scott in his book "An Experience Shared 1939-1945" quotes from the diary of Signalman Geoff Shaw who was on board the minelayer HMS ADVENTURE and witnessed the sinking.

"Mine exploded amidships under the tanker EMPIRE ROSEBERY. She split in two and both parts sunk. All that could be seen were the bows and stern jutting out of the water with a cluster of survivors in-between. No doubt someone rescued them - there were plenty of small craft pottering about. She sank in the time it took me to go into the signal distribution office, make an entry in the log, and come back out again."

In 1945 the MoWT acquired the American-built PINEBRANCH from Canadian owners, renamed her EMPIRE STICKLEBACK and placed her under Rowbotham management. Rowbotham was also allocated the management of two ex-German tankers taken as war reparations. Although allotted names it would appear they may not have actually been carried and only one served operationally, albeit briefly. One was the 800g DANISCH WOLD, allocated the name EMPIRE TIGLAS, while the other was the 1172g LISA ESSBERGER, allocated the name EMPIRE TEGENYA. DANISCH WOLD had been in St Malo in August 1944 when the Germans decided to move all useful vessels to Jersey for safety in the face of the American advance on the port. Laid up in Old Harbour at St Helier she was still there when the island was liberated by the British on 9th May 1945.

During the course of the war some of the managed vessels served in various theatres of operation, although not always under Rowbotham management. For instance, in 1942 EMPIRE LAD was carrying high octane aircraft fuel between the Clyde, Inverness and Scapa Flow. On 6th March, 1944, the allocation of several of these vessels was as follows:

| | |
|---|---|
| Petroleum Board | EMPIRE LAD, EMPIRE HOMESTEAD, EMPIRE BOXER, LOMA NOVIA and SAXET. |
| Admiralty | CHANT 25. |
| North Africa and Mediterranean | EMPIRE DAMSEL, EMPIRE LASS, MANNINGTON AND SALT CREEK. |
| Indian Ocean | TONKAWA. |
| Freetown | EMPIRE ARTHUR AND EMPIRE GYPSY. |

For Operation Overlord (D-Day) CHANTS 11, 12, 23 and 27, together with EMPIRE GYPSY, SAXET, LOMA NOVIA and EMPIRE ROSEBERY, were allocated to supply the combined armies in Normandy.

It was imperative that ships were prepared in time for the operation. However, there were delays and some did not meet their deadlines. On 5th June, 1944, Rowbotham replied to a letter from Captain "Dougie" Cable, who had been seconded to the Tanker Division of the MoWT from Bulk Oil Steamship Co. Ltd., noting that the following vessels should be ready for sea by the given dates:

| | |
|---|---|
| EMPIRE ROSEBERY | 25.6.44 |
| SAXET | 5.6.44 |
| SULPHUR BLUFF | 15.6.44 |
| LOMA NOVA | 5.6.44 |
| CHANT 23 | 5.6.44 |
| CHANT 27 | 5.6.44 |
| CHANT 11 | 20.6.44 |
| CHANT 12 | 26.6.44 |

Rowbotham indicated that the EMPIRE ROSEBERY would not be delivered from the builders before 10.7.44; alterations to SULPHUR BLUFF were in hand; CHANT 11 would be delivered by the builders on 14.6.44 and CHANT 12 on 24.6.44. The other vessels were ready for sea as required. The second part of the letter indicates operational requirements for the vessels as laid down by the MoWT.

"We confirm the following :-

(a) All vessels fitted with 6" stern discharge line.
(b) All vessels have been, or will be supplied with 90 fathoms 2" mooring wire.
(c) All vessels will have sufficient deck, engine room and cabin stores and equipment for three months.
(d) Flexible hose in all cases will be required to be brought up to 90 ft. on arrival at the operational loading station.
(e) Electrical stern signalling apparatus has been supplied to all vessels, with the exception of CHANT 23.
(f) Shapes and balls for daylight signalling have been ordered and will be put on board immediately.
(g) A sufficiency of portable fenders will be put on board all vessels. We also confirm that all fire-fighting equipment, anti-gas equipment, service respirators, steel helmets and first aid equipment have been made up in accordance with instructions."

Of the sixteen tugs managed by Rowbotham, in addition to those of the Overseas Towage & Salvage Co. Ltd., thirteen were wartime builds for the MoWT and carried out various tasks, principally naval duties or coastal towage. They came from three different classes of tug. The largest were of the 260g "Warrior" class (EMPIRE DEMON and EMPIRE FRANK) which were built primarily for river and estuary work. Of a similar type, but of 240g, were the four members of the "Birch" class (EMPIRE TEAK, EMPIRE RACE, EMPIRE MASCOT and EMPIRE LUCY). EMPIRE LUCY and EMPIRE RACE stayed under Rowbotham management until 1962 when they were sold to foreign buyers. One (EMPIRE DARBY) came from the "Modified Hornby" class of 203g tugs.

The smallest of the Empire tugs were of the 129g "Maple" class designed for dock and harbour work. Rowbotham managed six of this class of tug (EMPIRE CEDAR, EMPIRE FOLK, EMPIRE IMP, EMPIRE MAPLE, EMPIRE SERAPH and EMPIRE TOBY).

For a short time after the war Rowbotham managed three ex-German tugs which had been taken over as war reparation. They also retained the management of the 306g tanker NICKLEBY, ex EMPIRE NICKLEBY.

## Post-war expansion

One of the managed tankers, the 421d EMPIRE BOXER, was acquired by Rowbotham in 1946. She was renamed CHARTSMAN (I) and became the sixth member of the then current fleet. She was also the first of several post-war additions, all acquired second-hand. The second was the 586d HELMSMAN (III) bought in 1948. She was followed, in 1950, by the 504d BRIDGEMAN (I). In the following year the quartet was completed with the purchase of the 414d LEADSMAN (I), the war-time built and managed CHANT 11. As LEADSMAN (I) she became a frequent visitor to the Regent Oil wharf at Stockton. The first post-war new building came in 1953 when the company, in September of that year, took delivery of the 548d QUARTERMAN (I) from the yard of Clelands (Successors) Ltd. at Wallsend.

CHARTSMAN (I)                                          Andrew Huckett Collection

Until 1956 the company had been run as a partnership. William and Farnill Rowbotham had been joined in the company by their sons, Christopher, in 1925, and John, in 1931. Farnill died in 1943 and William in 1956, neither having formally retired. In 1956 Christopher bought out his cousin and converted the partnership into a limited company under the title of C. Rowbotham & Sons (Management) Ltd. Gradually the ships were transferred into the ownership of a variety of companies, with the parent company acting as manager. John Rowbotham left the company and his place was taken by his cousin Richard ("Dick") Rowbotham. Dick's father, the founder's third son, Stanley, had not entered the world of shipping but had qualified instead as a doctor.

1956 also saw the company's next acquisition, the 1934-built BASSETHOUND. Reconditioned by Drypool Engineering & Drydock Co. at Hull, and renamed POINTSMAN (I), she was time chartered to Shell-Mex and BP Ltd. and was mainly employed carrying boiler oil from the refinery at Stanlow to Herculaneum Dock Power Station. She was Rowbotham's first black oil carrier.

In 1958 Rowbotham placed an order with Drypool Engineering & Dry Dock Co. Ltd., Hull, for a new vessel. This was Drypool's first venture into ship-building, having been set up in 1921 as shiprepairers by the Rix family, coaster owners of Hull, for the repair of its own ships. A quotation had been obtained from Clelands (Successors) Ltd. of Wallsend but Drypool's proved cheaper. Completed at the beginning of the following year, the 1000d OARSMAN (I) was the first of six tankers built by Drypool for Rowbotham.

In 1962 Drypool undertook an extensive rebuild of the 1937-built HELMSMAN (III) which increased her deadweight capacity from 586 to 836 tons. Originally a trunk deck ship the rebuild consisted of flushing out the trunk which increased the draught of the ship by over 2 feet and the moulded depth by 4 feet. At the same time she received a new engine.

Of the five new buildings which joined the fleet between 1962 and 1967 the last to be completed was to be the largest vessel owned by the company to date and came from the yard of Clelands Shipbuilding Co. Ltd. at Wallsend. She was the 4574d WHEELSMAN (III). She was designed to the maximum dimensions to trade to a new depot opened by Regent Oil Co. Ltd. at Southwick, reached through the locks at Shoreham Harbour. For the time WHEELSMAN (III) embodied several new design features, which included a variable pitch propeller operated by a single lever from the bridge, a 65° wide-angle rudder, and large capacity pumps working in conjunction with 12" pumplines.

The fourth vessel, CHARTSMAN (II), was the company's first vessel to have bridge control and an unmanned engine room. In 1976 she was renamed RIVER LEE while on time charter to Texaco (Ireland) Ltd.

As the new building programme progressed over the years so did the disposal of older members of the fleet. This included CHARTSMAN (I) which, in 1966, was sold and as BAYMEAD, working out of Hayle in Cornwall, pioneered the extraction of tin from sea dredged material.

In concluding his articles for the company's house magazine, in October 1967, Dick Rowbotham commented on the diversified activities of the company. He wrote:

"The recent history of the firm would not be complete without mention of the remarkable expansion that has taken place in other directions in the last few years. Since the late 1950's the insurance interests have developed from a small broking company with a staff of about a dozen to six separate companies with a staff of nearly a hundred. Their activities now comprise all aspects of insurance - both broking and underwriting - on an international scale, and in terms of number of staff, the ships are now left far behind . . . This year has also seen the formation of the first Rowbotham Company outside the UK - Rowbotham Reinsurance (N. America) Inc., under the direction of John McCarthy in Boston - and this, with the Common Market in mind, may well be an indication of where the future lies. A little closer to home but still outside London, the firm is now represented on Merseyside by Willie Roberts, who is building up a thriving ship agency business in a part of the world where he has had many years experience."

By 1969 the total list of companies in The Rowbotham Group were as follows:

## Shipping Companies

C. Rowbotham & Sons (Management) Ltd.
The Helmsman Shipping Co. Ltd.
The Quarterman Shipping Co. Ltd.
C. Rowbotham & Sons (Chartering) Ltd.

## Ship Agency

W.J. Roberts & Son (Shipping) Ltd.

## Insurance Companies

C. Rowbotham & Sons (Insurance) Ltd.
C. Rowbotham & Sons (Underwriting Agency) Ltd.
Rowbotham (Reinsurance) Ltd.
Rowbotham Reinsurance (N. America) Inc.
Helmsman (Underwriting) Ltd.
Hargraves Bloch (Life and Pensions) Ltd.
A.J. Bell Ltd.

A further four vessels joined the fleet between 1968 and 1970. On delivery in 1970 the STEERSMAN (IV) was placed on a three month time charter to Esso Petroleum Co. Ltd. In 1976 she was renamed RIVER SHANNON on commencing a time charter to Texaco (Ireland) Ltd. With the departure of two vessels during this period, by the end of 1970, C. Rowbotham & Sons (Management) Ltd. managed ten tankers, all purpose built for the company.

RIVER SHANNON, ex Steersman (IV) at Milford Haven          Bernard McCall

## Sale to the Ingram Corporation

1970 proved to be a momentous year for Rowbotham. After trading as a family concern for 91 years, ever since Christopher Rowbotham first entered shipowning in 1879, the connection was severed when the total share capital of C. Rowbotham & Sons (Management) Ltd. was acquired by the Ingram Corporation of New Orleans. The decision to sell was made because the level of death duties which would be levied on the death of Christopher Rowbotham would be such as to decimate the company. The two alternatives were to become a public company or seek to sell to another company. At the time Rowbotham was advised that it should seek a buyer. Attempts were made to find a British buyer but without success. The sale, however, only concerned the shipping interests of the Rowbotham Group and the insurance side continued to function under family management. This was only until 1978 when the business was sold and all links with the Rowbotham family ceased.

The Ingram Corporation was founded in 1857 by O.H. Ingram. Like Christopher Rowbotham he came from humble origins, establishing a small sawmill on the banks of the Chippewa River in Wisconsin. The business grew with the acquisition of other timber companies in different parts of the United States. In 1938 I.H. Ingram, grandson of the founder, entered the oil industry with the establishment of the Wood River Oil and Refining Company. This concern grew until it possessed several producing properties, a refinery, a pipeline gathering system and river terminals, together with a fleet of barges to transport the company's products using inland waterways. In 1951 the majority of the assets of the company were acquired by a major oil company. Retaining only two river terminals and a small fleet of towboats and barges, O.H. Ingram created another refining and marketing enterprise, which was named the Ingram Oil & Refining Company. Expansion took place with the establishment of a refinery, further river terminals and service stations in the south eastern states. In 1961 Ingram Oil merged with the Murphy Oil Corporation but the waterborne petroleum facilities were retained in Ingram hands and formed into the Ingram Barge Company which, in 1962, became the operating division of the Ingram Corporation. Expansion continued in the area of marine transportation and through its subsidiaries and divisions it was able to transport large quantities of sand, gravel and rock as well as petroleum and petro-chemical products. The acquisition of Rowbotham was their first venture outside of the United States.

In 1971 Rowbotham moved out of the offices occupied in the Minories to offices at 100 Fenchurch Street. During the following year they moved out of London altogether, to Abbey House in Farnborough, Hampshire. There they stayed for seven years.

Under the direction of their new parent company Rowbotham entered a new period of expansion. The 1972-built petroleum product tankers HELMSMAN (IV) and BRIDGEMAN (II) were joined in the following year by the chemical tankers ASTRAMAN and POLARISMAN. These two tankers pioneered Rowbotham's entry into a new area of trade, that of the transportation of chemicals in specially designed vessels to distribution points throughout the country and mainland Europe. They were designed to conform to the Inter-Govermental Maritime Consultative Organisation's new regulations concerning the prevention of pollution from ships and were the first ships to be built in the UK to this new specification. IMCO has since been renamed the International Maritime Organisation (IMO).

In October 1971 the IMCO Assembly adopted a Code for the Construction and Equipment of Ships Carrying Dangerous Chemicals in Bulk. The Code designated three types of vessels, type 1 being designed and equipped for the carriage of chemicals which required maximum preventative measures to prevent their escape and to survive significant collision and stranding damage, while types 2 and 3 were designed for the carriage of less hazardous chemicals. ASTRAMAN and POLARISMAN were built as IMCO Type 1 chemical tankers. They were fitted with a total of five centre and eight wing tanks, four of the centre tanks being suitable for the carriage of type 1 chemicals, with the wing tanks forming a double skin and the fifth centre tank acting as a cofferdam. They had a double bottom which extended the full length of the cargo space, and were fitted with segregated systems of lines and pumps for cargo work and water ballast, plus a tank ventilation system with separate lines running from each cargo tank to the fore part of the ship. Ventilation could either take place into the atmosphere or into a tank for the cargo vapour to be disposed of ashore. Although Rowbotham pioneered the way in building these tankers to IMCO's highest standards, the higher cost involved was probably not justified in view of the small quantities of the most hazardous chemicals being conveyed by sea. Later chemical tankers were built to IMCO type 2 and 3 standards.

A third ship delivered in 1973 was the 2050d petroleum tanker QUARTERMAN (II), constructed principally to service the Northern Ireland port of Carrickfergus. This year also saw the departure of the 1959-built OARSMAN (I) for conversion into a sand dredger.

In 1974 the Ingram Corporation expanded its European operations by acquiring two additional, very different, companies. One was the Humber-based shipbuilders Richard Dunston Industries Ltd., which was acquired by Ingram's British subsidiary, Ingram Maritime Co. Ltd. Dunston operated two shipyards, one at Hessle and the other at Thorne. The Hessle yard specialised in building coastal and short sea trade vessels, tugs and barges. They had already built QUARTERMAN (II) for Rowbotham and were later to build two further small tankers for the company. The Thorne yard built smaller vessels such as tugs, trawlers, hoppers, barges, utility boats and small naval patrol craft. The company stayed in Ingram's ownership until November 1986 when it was bought out by a management team. In March 1988 Richard Dunston (Hessle) Ltd. became a wholly owned subsidiary of the Dutch Damen Shipyards of Gorinchem. It went into liquidation in December 1994.

The second acquisition was the Swiss-based Tampimex Holding A.G. which was a holding company for an international, independent oil trading group. It began with a company formed in Berlin in 1921 and expanded with the establishing of Tampimex Oil Products Ltd. in London in 1936. At that time the company was mainly engaged in the purchase and sale of bitumen from Tampico, Mexico, which gave rise to its name. They later expanded into trading in bulk oil and products which developed into the main activity of the group. At the time of acquisition the group was made up of subsidiary companies in Hamburg, Zurich, New York and Houston as well as in London.

On behalf of Ingram Tankships Ltd. & Tampimex Oil Ltd., Rowbotham acted as technical advisers and managers for two product carriers which did not form part of the coastal fleet. These were the 29,999d OSCO INGRAM OSPREY, completed in July 1982, and the 32,259d OSCO TAMPIMEX EAGLE, which had been completed in January 1977 as NORDIC AURORA.

In 1975 the 6176d ORIONMAN was delivered by Hall, Russell & Co. Ltd., Aberdeen. A chemical tanker, she became, for a time, the largest member of the Rowbotham fleet.

In the following year four pure chemical tankers joined the ever increasing fleet. These were the 2324d STELLAMAN (I) and MARSMAN and the 3560d CENTAURMAN and VEGAMAN. The latter two vessels were renamed ESSEX TROPHY and ESSEX TRIUMPH briefly in 1983 while on charter to Midship Maritime (Gibraltar) Ltd. The name ESSEX TROPHY was never officially recorded by Lloyd's Register, but there is photographic evidence that CENTAURMAN did carry the name, if only for a short while. Due to a deterioration in the chemical market, as a result of the depressed economic situation prevailing at the time, and the resultant over tonnage in chemical tankers, plus the fact that Rowbotham was not a dedicated chemical carrying company, led to the decision to sell the four ships en bloc to Buries Markes Ltd. in 1987. The other chemical tankers were retained because of their ability to carry petroleum products.

STELLAMAN (I)                                                                    WSS

In 1979 the company left Farnborough and returned to London, taking over offices in Bush House in the Aldwych.

After a gap of four years, in 1980, two contrasting ships were added to the fleet. These were the 2547d OARSMAN and the much larger CABLEMAN at 8000d.

On 1st January, 1981, there was a change in the company's name, C. Rowbotham & Sons (Management) Ltd. becoming Rowbotham Tankships Ltd.

No Rowbotham tanker went to the Falklands during the conflict in 1982. However, CABLEMAN and TANKERMAN were chartered for a time to the Ministry of Defence and TANKERMAN did get as far as Ascension Island.

1982 saw another expansion in the fleet with the delivery of two new vessels. On entering service the 6125d ECHOMAN was almost immediately placed on a Gulf Oil charter, operating out of Milford Haven to Eastham, Cardiff and Avonmouth, until replaced by her slightly larger sister, CABLEMAN, in January 1987. The second vessel was the 1563d OILMAN.

ECHOMAN at Falmouth in November 1990                Ambrose Greenway

## Acquisitions

However, these were not Rowbotham's only acquisition in this year. In October 1982, they acquired three companies of the Humber-based Sir Fred Parkes group from Turnbull Scott Management Ltd. These were Hull Gates Shipping Co. Ltd., Hull Gates Shipping Management Ltd., and the ship agency S.F. Craggs & Co. Ltd. Turnbull Scott had taken over the whole group in 1981 although it continued to operate in its own right. In the following year it disposed of the shipping interests within the group to Rowbotham. Overnight the Rowbotham fleet increased by nine vessels - three fully owned, two on bareboat charters and four managed. The oldest was the 1969-built, 2861d, HUMBERGATE. Of the four Japanese-built sisters, EASTGATE and WESTGATE, both built in 1979, were fully owned, while the 1980-built NORTHGATE and 1981-built IRISHGATE were on bareboat charter. The four small Japanese-built sisters, STEN, PER, CHRISTIAN and NATALIE, only remained under Rowbotham management for a year.

WESTGATE was not in the UK when Rowbotham took over Hull Gates. At the time she was in the middle of what turned out to be a six year charter to Ethioship, trading to Ethiopia and around the Red Sea with petroleum products from the refinery at Aden. On completion of the charter in December 1987, while en route back to the UK, she was diverted to the Gulf and taken on charter by the United States' Military Sealift Command. Based at Bahrain she spent six months bunkering United States' warships patrolling the Gulf during the Iran-Iraq war.

The company's last new building for ten years came out in 1983. She was the 10716d TANKERMAN. In the same year three older members left the fleet, while the company moved offices again. This time it was to No 7 St. James' Square, Pall Mall, where they stayed for three years.

On 15th June, 1984, tragedy struck Rowbotham Tankships when an explosion occurred on board POINTSMAN. While lying at Milford Docks, undergoing routine repairs to a pump room valve, an explosion took place caused by the ignition of gas. The ship had received a gas free certificate allowing burning work to take place on board. In this initial explosion two crew members were killed as well as two employees of the Milford Dock Company. In two further explosions a total of seventeen people were injured, including fire-fighters from the local fire brigade and ambulancemen. POINTSMAN was subsequently taken to Cardiff for repairs.

On the day POINTSMAN left Milford Haven, 21st June, QUARTERMAN suffered a gearbox failure while approximately 10 miles off Holyhead. At the time she was en route from Milford Haven to Workington with a cargo of pre-mium motor spirit. RIVER SHANNON, en route in ballast to Milford Haven, diverted and towed the disabled vessel to Liverpool where she was repaired.

Due to a financial crisis, in 1985, the Ingram Corporation was advised by its bankers, the First National Bank of Chicago, to sell Rowbotham Tankships, this being the only financially viable part of the Ingram Corporation. It was acquired by another United States company, the New Jersey-based Marine Transport Lines Inc.

During the 15 years that Rowbotham was owned by the Ingram Corporation there had been many significant advances in the company. Nearly all of the company's older tonnage had been replaced by new vessels, seventeen being built during this period. The company had entered the chemical trade. Its fleet had been further increased with the take over of the Hull Gates' ships. Its technical expertise had been used in the building of two product carriers. Its headquarters had moved several times but was now established back in London. The advances that had been made by the company, while still under family control, had been built upon making Rowbotham Tankships Ltd. the largest short sea tanker company in the UK.

## Marine Transport Lines

The pedigree of Marine Transport Lines was even longer than that of Rowbotham or Ingram, and, again, was the result of a family enterprise which set up its first company in 1760. The Mallory family began as sail makers. In 1822 Charles Mallory entered shipowning through the whaling industry. The company later moved into sailing tramps and packets and then into steam. In the early years of this century it ran the New York & Texas Steamship Company. Prior to the First World War it operated a fleet of 70 steamers operating under the names of Clyde Line, Mallory Line, Porto Rico Line and Ward Line. After being served by six generations of Mallorys the company was taken over by the GATX Corporation in 1941. It was later to become a public company. At the time of its acquisition of Rowbotham Tankships, Marine Transport Lines still maintained a heavy involvement in shipping. It owned and managed a varied fleet of about 28 vessels which included tankers and product carriers, bulk carriers and car carriers. Rowbotham Tankships was its first venture into the European market.

In 1986 Rowbotham moved into offices at Glen House, Stag Place, in the City of Westminster.

During the 1980s many shipping companies sought to make savings in their operational costs by flagging their ships away from the state flag to offshore registers. The principal savings were in the lower costs involved in registering ships with offshore registers and crew-related expenses. In January 1987, Rowbotham Tankships announced that it was to transfer its then fleet of twenty-three vessels to the Isle of Man register. As part of the process all sea-going staff were offered new employment contracts with Marine Manning Services Ltd. of Hong Kong. The crew management contract for the fleet was placed with Wallem Ship Management (Isle of Man) Ltd., an associate company of Marine Manning Services. Unlike many other shipping companies Rowbotham Tankships continued to maintain existing manning levels and to crew their ships with British seafarers.

By the end of 1987 the Rowbotham fleet had decreased to nineteen vessels from its peak of twenty-six ships at the time of the acquisition by Marine Transport Lines. This was due to the departure of three of the 1960s built oil tankers and the four chemical tankers.

In 1989 two new vessels joined the fleet, both second-hand purchases, these being renamed GUIDESMAN (III) and TILLERMAN (III). This latter vessel, at 12800d, was by far the largest vessel operated by Rowbotham Tankships.

## New owners

In 1989 another change took place in the parent company. In June of that year a management buy out was launched for Marine Transport Lines by three of its directors, including the company's chairman, Karl Meyer. The bid was unsuccessful. However, a counter bid from the newly established Intrepid Acquisition Corporation, under the chairmanship of Richard du Moulin, was accepted. So, on 13th October, 1989, Marine Transport Lines again became a private company. It was soon announced by the new parent company that they intended to seek partners for joint ventures in its various operations and, in particular, one for its European subsidiary, Rowbotham Tankships Ltd.

This came about on 3rd May, 1990, when P&O Bulk Shipping Ltd. acquired 50% of the assets of Rowbotham Tankships. P&O paid a reported £11.2 million and became joint partners with Marine Transport Lines in Rowbotham. This was a return by P&O into involvement with coastal tankers after their previous ownership of the chemical tankers PASS OF DRUMOCHTER and PASS OF DIRRIEMORE. Mr Karl Timmermann, managing director of P&O Bulk Shipping, became first chairman of the jointly owned company. Mr Albert Shaw, who had been initially appointed in 1989, remained as managing director, being succeeded on his retirement, in June 1991, by Mr Nick Josephy.

In June 1991 Rowbotham Tankships announced that they had signed a contract with Malaysia Shipyard & Engineering Sdn. Bhd., Johore, for two 6200d clean petroleum product carriers for delivery in 1992/3. The order was later increased to four vessels with delivery of the second two being 1993/4. In the event delivery was late. These vessels, the first new buildings for the company since the delivery of TANKERMAN in 1983, were also the first double-hulled vessels in the fleet with five completely segregated cargo tanks offering a large cubic to deadweight capacity. They were also fitted with 10 deepwell pumps of 350 cubic metre an hour capacity to ensure rapid loading and discharge. In 1993, prior to the delivery of the first vessel, it was announced that they would be registered in Liberia, the first vessels in the company's history not to fly the Red Ensign. The first of the new buildings, ANCHORMAN (II), was delivered in July 1993 and sailed for the UK with a complement of British officers and Filipino crew. By this time the registered owners of the four vessels were several investment partnerships based in Nordenham in Germany.

A dispute with the builders soon arose in which Rowbotham maintained that the four tankers suffered from unpredictable manoeuvring which could result in an oil spill. The problem was resolved by modifying the single-rudder steering gear to a twin-rudder configuration. The costs incurred in this modification, plus loss of earnings while the work was carried out, led to substantial damages being claimed against Malaysia Shipyard and Engineering. These were disputed and the matter became a subject of litigation.

## Contract of Affreightment operations

After the cessation of the Second World War, and the de-merger of the Petroleum Board, Rowbotham had pursued a unique trading strategy, developed by Christopher Rowbotham, of conducting a Contract of Affreightment operation. This is a particular chartering agreement whereby charterers agree to offer, and shipowners agree to carry, so many tons of cargo between agreed loading and discharging ports, over a specific period of time, usually of 12 months, with an option to renew, at agreed rates of freight per ton. Cargoes are nominated by charterers at an agreed minimum notice, and owners agree to load in an agreed span of lay-days/cancelling. All other charter party details are included within the agreement.

While other companies secured time charters with the major oil companies, Rowbotham's operation was founded on two basic Contracts of Affreightment agreements with Regent Oil and Petrofina. During the 1950s and 1960s new Contracts of Affreightment were secured with new entrants into the UK oil market - Conoco (Jet), Amoco, Murco, Phillips and Gulf Oil. To service these contracts, whilst awaiting delivery of new tonnage, Rowbotham chartered in tonnage to a considerable degree. Although the company always maintained a large Contract of Affreightment operation time charters also played a major part in chartering activities, as did spot charters to a lesser extent.

## Ports and registrations

At sometime or the other Rowbotham ships have been found in almost every oil port around the UK and Irish coast and also in north-west Europe. Latterly, its principal loading ports have been Milford Haven, in West Wales, with its refineries belonging to Texaco and Elf (previously Amoco), and the now closed Esso and Gulf refineries; and Immingham, on the River Humber, with its Conoco and Lindsay (Petrofina/Total) refineries. From these, and other refineries and ocean storage terminals, Rowbotham vessels served many sea-fed depots to which they sailed for the discharge of their cargoes. Sometimes, however, charters have taken vessels further afield. WESTGATE operated in the Red Sea and the Gulf. POINTSMAN spent several years in the Caribbean on charter to Texaco. She is also believed to be the only Rowbotham vessel to traverse both the Suez and Panama canals. CENTAURMAN and VEGAMAN operated for Pemex in Mexico. IRISHGATE found its way to West Africa. Several ships have operated into the Baltic.

In anticipation of the liberalising of the European Union cabotage trades, in March 1992 Rowbotham announced that it was to re-register its fleet. This move was necessary as the Isle of Man is not a full member of the European Union. Fifteen of the product tankers went to the Gibraltar register while the three chemical tankers, not eligible for registration in Gibraltar, went to the Hong Kong register. Under a 1987 law, Gibraltar was not permitted to register certain types of vessels, including chemical tankers. At the same time as the re-registration the crew management contract for the ships passed to Pentmarine (1982) Ltd. of Hong Kong.

During 1992 five of the older members of the fleet were sold to new owners. This brought the fleet down to fifteen vessels prior to the delivery of the new buildings. To supplement its own tonnage the company took on time charter the 9441d HYDRO, owned by Hydroship A/S of Sweden.

On 15th January, 1993, P&O purchased Marine Transport Lines' 50% interest in Rowbotham Tankships Ltd. With the company now under total P&O ownership its name was changed to that of P&O Tankships Ltd., a subsidiary of P&O Bulk Shipping Ltd. Along with the change in ownership there was a change in the fleet's livery to that of corporate P&O. There was no policy to rename the ships so they retained their traditional Rowbotham nomenclature. The company's office was moved to the LWT Building, Upper Ground, London SE1, to share with P&O Bulk Shipping Ltd.

At the time of its take over, P&O announced expansion plans which were intended to see a return to the chemical trade, probably through the acquisition of another company, and the ordering of new tonnage. By 1994 the four new buildings ordered by Rowbotham had entered service and the 3600d NAVAJO had been purchased and renamed STELLAMAN (II). The sale of older members of the fleet had continued with the departure of four vessels in 1994, and two in 1995. One of these was the 1972-built ASTRAMAN, at the time the oldest member of the fleet.

## Sale to Fishers

In October 1994, P&O Tankships announced the awarding of a contract for four 3700d double-hulled product carriers to the Qiuxin Shipyard in Shanghai. The contract was awarded against tough international competition via the state-controlled China Shipbuilding Trading Co. This was Qiuxin's first order for a European buyer, and would be the first Chinese-built ships to be exported directly to the UK. The first of the quartet, QUARTERMAN (III), was launched in January 1996. Like the Malaysian-built vessels they were to be fitted with high capacity pumps and a combination of bow thrusters and twin rudders for greater manoeuvrability.

In November 1996 it was reported that the Malaysian company Konsortium Parkapalan Berhad was interested in purchasing P&O Tankships. However, only a week later it was announced that James Fisher and Sons Public Limited Company, of Barrow in Furness, were to buy the company, a sale concluded on Monday 30th December for the reported sum of £38.8 million.

At the time of the acquisition P&O Tankships were operating seventeen clean product tankers, ten owned, four on long-term bareboat charter and three on annual charters. These were HYDRO, Dublin Shipping's RATHKYLE, ex RICH STAR-87 (IRL, 8162g/81), and James Fisher's MICHAEL M, ex BP HUNTER-91 (GBR, 2077g/80).

With the renaming of the company to that of James Fisher Tankships Ltd., the adoption of a new houseflag and funnel markings, the sale of the ECHOMAN in 1997, the renaming of the China-built vessels, and, in 1998, the renaming of two existing members of the fleet, the demise of the Rowbotham identity is almost complete.

MILFORD FISHER at Jersey                              Dave Hocquard

However, the legacy of Christopher Rowbotham continues. From small beginnings what became a family concern grew into a highly respected shipping company operating in the short sea trade. With the opening up of the single market for the European short sea trades in 1997 the opportunities for an enterprising company are enormous. Such opportunities were seen by Christopher Rowbotham in his day, as they are by his successors today, who also see future opportunities, particularly with the ending of cabotage and a change in the national preference policies operated by some European state oil companies. Christopher Rowbotham's legacy has been inherited by James Fisher as it seeks to continue to exploit the market of which it is an integral part.

# STEERSMAN (III)
by
Captain John Harvey

I joined STEERSMAN as an ordinary seaman at Goole in January 1937, when I was 15 years of age. Serving under Captain H. Triggs, we traded home and continental carrying mainly petrol. At that time STEERSMAN was Rowbotham's biggest ship, with a cargo capacity of 414 tons, in six divided tanks, overall length being 152 feet. Before that a steam STEERSMAN had been trading out of Goole, but was scrapped and this new motorship built. Rowbotham were a very good company to be in. The boss was a Mr Christopher Rowbotham, affectionately called by all his employees "Chris", though as far as I can remember no one ever met him. We frequently went to the captain for our weekly wage and afterwards were called back to be given another one, a gift from "Chris", and at Christmas we all received an extra week's wage as bonus (my weekly wage was then £2.7.6).

STEERSMAN (III)                                                                    WSPL

In 1938 when the Second World War seemed imminent we were ordered to proceed to Saltend to load a cargo of aviation spirit for HMS ARK ROYAL at Rosyth, and we arrived at Rosyth, moored to a buoy, awaiting the arrival of the carrier. In the meantime Mr Chamberlain returned from Berlin proclaiming "peace in our time", and we never discharged our cargo, but returned it to Saltend.

When war eventually did break out we were loading spirit at Coryton in the Thames, and at 11.10 am after hearing the war declaration, we started painting our lovely white superstructure grey.

I remember going to Jersey, and in those days we had no radio transmitter so did not know that the invasion of the islands was imminent until someone signalled from a cliff top, with a single flag morse code telling us to leave the area. Another of our ships, the WHEELSMAN, was discharging petrol at the time, but he ceased operations and left with quite a few of the locals on board. We eventually went up to Scotland, supplying the RAF fighter station at Inverness with spirit from Bowling on the Clyde.

One Sunday we were passing along the Caledonian Canal with a cargo of aviation spirit for Inverness. We had left Kitra lock and were about half way to Fort Augustus locks when a German bomber attacked us, dropping one bomb only. It fell into the canal just astern of the ship but did not explode. We were told that the pilot had not allowed for the fact that we were 100 feet above sea level. His sights were set for sea level, consequently the bomb fell a few feet away. It was a beautiful sunny day about 1 pm.

In 1941, when on passage from Bowling to Douglas, Isle of Man, shortly after leaving the river but while still in the estuary, we suffered a massive collision. When I dashed on deck in pitch darkness there was a submarine with a searchlight trained on us, and I feared the worst, but no, it was in fact one of ours escorting a French destroyer. It was the destroyer who had collided with us, almost tearing the port side out of us, and spilling spirit everywhere, but luckily there was no explosion or fire despite a massive display of huge sparks. That proved to be the beginning of the end of my connection with Rowbotham, because repairs were estimated to take three months. We went to Newport, then Cardiff, and finally Swansea before a repair yard accepted us. All hands, except Captain Triggs, were paid off. It was a sad day for us all, because we had all sailed together all the time. I was an AB by then and studying for my tickets.

[Captain J. Harvey retired in 1991 after 54 years at sea, the last 30 years as a home trade master.]

STEERSMAN (III)                                                                    WSPL

# EMPIRE DAMSEL

by

Robert Sutherland

[Mr Sutherland signed on the EMPIRE DAMSEL in Glasgow, on 14th May, 1943, as Radio Operator (Foreign-going Articles). The crew consisted of the master, two deck officers, one radio officer, three engineers, a steward and deck boy, four to six ABs, three greasers, one DEMS gunlayer and three ratings.

EMPIRE DAMSEL was armed with one 12-pounder dual purpose gun, two 20mm Oerlikons, two twin Marlin .303 machine guns plus several smoke cannisters.

Mr Sutherland's allocated "action station" was the bridge port side Marlin which meant he had to lengthen the telephone leads so as to keep wireless watch as well.]

After several days finishing odd jobs and storing ship, we sailed in convoy for Algiers. About two days out we ran into a storm and were unable to keep up with the convoy. We returned to the Clyde and were then ordered to Milford Haven to join a coastal convoy to Plymouth. After about a week we received orders to join a LCT (Landing Craft Tank) convoy for Gibraltar. From being the smallest ship in the first convoy we now became the largest. The convoy was composed of about 30 LCTs, 12 MFVs (motor fishing vessels), several boom defence vessels and a couple of Dutch tugs under escort of half a dozen trawlers.

It was a quiet voyage to Gibraltar. After loading aviation spirit we sailed in convoy to Malta. We were impressed with the escort of seven full size destroyers after seeing the usual Western Ocean Group. While rounding Cape Bon we came under attack from a number of German aircraft. I seem to remember we spent most of an afternoon under attack. There was one curious incident. During the bombing one of the escort apparently obtained an echo on his asdic and dropped a number of depth charges. Lo and behold up from the bottom rises a vessel which immediately bursts into flame. We were on the other side of the convoy but it did not look like a submarine or anything we could recognise. It was thought probably to have been a German fuel barge sunk during the evacuation of Tunisia. The thick black smoke from this hung over the convoy and possibly helped to hide us from attack during the night.

On arrival in Malta we anchored in St. Paul's Bay staying there for about a week before transferring to Sliema Creek. We now found out that our purpose in life was to refuel Coastal Forces' MTBs (motor torpedo boats), MGBs (motor gun boats) and such like. While in Sliema Creek a number of LCIs (Landing Craft Infantry) (loaded with 51st Division personnel) tied alongside. This was the first definite news we had of Operation Husky (the invasion of Sicily). We were not to go with the first wave. For the next two days we got a series of contradictory orders - sail-don't sail-sail-don't sail - the reason for which became apparent when HMS INDOMITABLE came into port having been torpedoed and we were required to take off all her aviation spirit. This done we then sailed for Augusta in Sicily.

We arrived as it got dark and anchored among a group of merchant ships. The air raids started at about 10 o'clock and seemed to go on most of the night. With our limited armament there was little we could do apart from assisting with smoke generation. Early in the morning, after dawn had broken but with the smoke still hanging around, there was a tremendous explosion and one of the merchant ships (a "Fort" boat we thought) which had been on fire blew up. This vessel was at the far end of the anchorage from us and we could not assist in any way. The day light air raids now started and this meant we were on standby all day. The following night two further merchant ships were hit and commenced to burn. These ships were all combat-loaded and all night they erupted fire and explosions, fortunately not like their sister of the previous night. In the morning a Greek destroyer fired numerous shells at their waterlines, in the hope of quenching the flames. All undamaged ships, apart from us, were now ordered to Syracuse. This left Augusta relatively empty apart from two cruisers and several destroyers and coastal forces.

We got another anchorage towards the north end of the harbour and commenced fuelling MTBs. About this time we saw the EMPIRE LASS and paid a visit. I think they had been out since the original landing in North Africa and had been having a dodgy time sailing between Algiers and Bone. Anyway now we had arrived they sailed to Malta and we did not see them again.

This first visit we spent about three weeks in Augusta until our cargo was exhausted. We then returned to Malta to reload. Augusta was not a very nice place to be in with numerous raids every day and most nights. We used to cheer ourselves by saying that we were too small to bother with and the targets were the cruisers NEWFOUNDLAND, MAURITIUS, ORION and two large monitors.

The second spell in Augusta I cannot speak about as I spent the time ashore in the hospital rejoining the ship just in time to return to Malta.

After loading we returned to Augusta in time to sail for Messina which had been captured. The Coastal Forces' base had been shifted there and we, of course, went with it. About this time there were big doings in the Mediterranean - surrender of Italy - landing at Salerno - and our small part of the action started about 28th September. Coastal Forces had again decided to shift, this time to Maddalena - an Italian base on the island between Corsica and Sardinia. Consequently an odd convoy assembled consisting of EMPIRE DAMSEL, two LCTs containing the base and stores, heavily escorted by half a dozen MTBs and MGBs. The weather turned bad and we sheltered in Milazzo, then on to Palermo. Eventually on to Sardinia. The latter part of the voyage meant crawling along as close to the Sardinian coast and inside small islands as this base had been heavily mined and a full sweep had not been carried out.

At Maddalena we were able to discharge into shore tanks and, awaiting the unloading of the LCTs, we set off again. The LCTs left us when abeam of Palermo but we carried on to Bizerta. There we loaded again and returned to Maddalena. This was the last of our Coastal Forces trips and we now became an ordinary coastal tanker in which one voyage melted into the next.

Trips performed included those between Algiers and Bone (often), Bizerta and Palermo. There was one voyage from Bizerta to Porto Empedocle (Sicily) in which a rain squall blotted out the convoy we were about to join and we collided with our next ahead who had stopped. We hit his cruiser stern and this cut into our messroom nearly to the waterline. We were able to complete our voyage and after discharging were sent to Oran for repair. Our priority was low and it took about six weeks before we were fit again.

Christmas was spent loading in Ferryville (Lac de Bizerta). We also made a trip between Oran and Tunis and in 1944 we actually got out of the Mediterranean as far as Casablanca. The swept channel for Casablanca was about 10 to 15 miles west of the port. This bothered the anti-submarine aircraft who had to take two runs at us during the night to make sure who we were.

On the way back we had to call at Gibraltar to join a convoy. When lowering the boat at Gibraltar it took the davits with it. A passing boom defence vessel fished them from the bottom and they were rewelded before we could sail.

Algiers to Bone seemed to be our favourite grounds. Much quieter than it had been but the Luftwaffe still paid a lot of attention to convoys off the North African coast. We went to Brindisi to dry dock. This was shortly after the dreadful air raid on Bari where so many were killed and the mustard gas released. It was quite a topic of conversation at the time but did not seem to hit the history books.

On D-Day (6 June 1944) I recall sailing down the channel to Ferryville.

Towards the middle of July we were in Algiers to change the crew. All changed except the skipper and I. The skipper was William Gilchrist - a thorough gentleman and a pleasure to sail with. The replacement ABs were mostly Spanish, a scratch lot several of whom had never been to sea before. At the time it was said they were all refugees from France. The ship was fumigated at the time and we were all boarded ashore. If we could be said to have a home port in the Mediterranean it would be Algiers. Even there it was in-load-sail as quickly as possible. If there was no convoy due they would send us off with a trawler or whatever was available. In 1944 we found trips on our own were usually quiet whereas a convoy could almost depend on some attention.

On leaving Algiers loaded we went to Ajaccio. After discharging we returned to North Africa (Bizerta I think) and loaded for Maddalena. At Maddelena we got word of the forthcoming invasion of the south of France and that we were to be a small part of it back in our original role of refuelling Coastal Forces.

The day before D-Day we left Maddelena and anchored in a small bay off the north west coast of Sardinia to await our LST (Landing Ship Tank) convoy which was coming from Naples through the Bonifacio Straits. It turned up on time - we attached ourselves to the tail end and off we went to practice our French.

Not having any charts we were a bit lost when we got to the French coast but we thought if we kept close to the American headquarters ship (USS ANCON) someone would be bound to notice us. As invasions went this was a bit of a non-starter, some gunfire on D-Day and the odd plane. In spite of our precautions it was two days before we were found and ordered to anchor off Hyeres. I do not think Coastal Forces were overpowered by work. Eventually we moved to St. Tropez and lay there for about two weeks. Thence to Toulon to finish discharging. From there to Naples where the skipper and I signed off on 16th October, 1944.

# NICKLEBY
by
John C. Bellaby

The ship I served in was the NICKLEBY, ex EMPIRE NICKLEBY, built by Isaac Pimblott & Sons Ltd. at Northwich on the River Weaver. She was 127 feet overall, 107 net tons, capacity of 300 tons. She had a huge six-cylinder diesel that was really too powerful, and allegedly war surplus and not really meant for the ship. The crew was supposed to number nine but was actually seven. The master and the mate were Rowbotham men from Goole, the chief engineer a very handsome ladies' man, a greaser, the cook, a first tripper from the army, and two ABs, one of them being me! We often met with other ships of the company, all regular vessels with names like TILLERMAN and RUDDERMAN.

She was my first (and only) coaster and I can honestly state that I learned more, worked harder, and was sometimes more scared than at any other period of my time at sea.

I joined the ship at Preston in July 1946. We sailed early the next morning for Stanlow and thence to the Bristol Channel. During the next three months we were constantly at sea except for two days wind-bound in Swansea. We carried every kind of oil product there was - petrol, lubricating oil, aviation spirit, gas oil, paraffin. We docked, many times, in Avonmouth, Cardiff, Barry, Swansea, Hayle, Hamble and Portslade on the south coast, Falmouth, Malpas, Coryton, and paid off in Rotherhithe on 5th October.

We steered by quarter-points. The wheel was almost five feet across and protruded forward of the steering box. This made viewing the compass and controlling the wheel almost impossible. The steering was completely 'hand-draulic'. There was no hydraulic assistance, no buffers to absorb kick-backs. It was usual in very bad weather (and we had plenty) to be pushed over 180° off course and sometimes be catapulted right over the wheel. Despite the power of the engine we often went astern trying to make headway. It once took almost twelve hours to pass Hartland Point after leaving Cardiff. Many times we ran for Lundy and sheltered in its lee. The skipper did everything to keep a schedule. We would go down the Bristol Channel from our last port hugging the shoreline using the ebb to give us more speed. If our engine had failed we would have been left high and dry! Rounding Lands End we always went inside the Longships - whatever the weather. If you have never sailed up the Usk in pouring rain at five on a Sunday morning, and had to come alongside a broken down old wharf that was not safe to walk on, never mind tie up to, then you do not know to what depths your morale can sink.

The generator was never operated in port. This meant that coming back aboard in the pitch dark, feeling one's way down ladders and along alleyways could be an interesting experience!

Sometimes all of us up on the bridge were violently sick in bad weather, master, mate and we two ABs. We worked extremely hard and very long hours, the pay, for the time, was good, the food passable. The thing I missed was sufficient reading matter as there was no onboard library. However, all the time I was with the NICKLEBY our mail found us, no matter where we docked, and well on time too. Obviously someone in Rowbotham's office was well organised and had our welfare at heart.

# FLEET LISTS

Unless otherwise stated, all vessels are tankers.
For notes see inside back cover

## OWNED SHIPS

**1. PRINCESS** 1879-1917 Wooden ketch

O.N. 67828. 100g, 100n. 78.0 x 21.4 x 9.9 feet.

*4.1879:* Launched by William Wake, Goole for Christopher Rowbotham, George James King and William Andrews, Goole. *1898:* All shares in the vessel acquired by Christopher Rowbotham. *1908:* Owners became C. Rowbotham & Sons. *1917:* Sold to J.W. Raddings, Kingston upon Hull. *22.3.1917:* Left Hull for Guernsey with a cargo of coal and subsequently foundered off the coast of Norfolk with the loss of her crew of four.

**2. ATHLETAE** 1885-1890 Wooden schooner

O.N. 54517. 109n. 85.4 x 21.6 x 10.7 feet.

*7.1867:* Launched by William Wake, Goole for W. Cass, Goole. *1885:* Acquired by Christopher Rowbotham. *25.1.1890:* While on a voyage from Leith to Woolwich Arsenal, with a cargo of Government stores and iron, she was abandoned at sea during a gale off the coast of Yorkshire.

**3. ELSIE** 1889-1905 Wooden schooner

O.N. 96593. 165g, 147n. 104.6 x 25.0 x 10.1 feet.

From *1920:* 2-cyl. direct acting vertical paraffin engine by H. Weddop & Co., Keighley.

*1876:* Completed by R. Moller, Faaborg for N.R. Storm, Denmark as THUSNELDA. *1889:* Acquired by Christopher Rowbotham and renamed ELSIE. *1905:* Sold to Robert C. Roberts, Manchester. *1908:* Sold to Coppack Brothers & Co., Connah's Quay. *1910:* Owners became Thomas Coppack & Co., Connah's Quay. *1916:* Sold to William A. Jenkins, Swansea. *1920:* Sold to Stephen and Ruth Chugg, Braunton, Devon. *1925:* Broken up.

### 4. CELESTINA 1890-1904 Wooden schooner

O.N. 95111. 115g, 99n. 92.0 x 22.4 x 9.8 feet.

2.*1889:* Completed by W.H. Lean, Falmouth for Timothy White, Sandport. *1890:* Acquired by Christopher Rowbotham. *1904:* Sold to John Winship, Barton-on-Humber. *1.10.1911:* While at anchor in the River Thames, during a voyage from Par to London with a cargo of china clay, she parted cables and drove across Pan Sand. Having got sail on she made for Dover. Near North Spit off Margate she rolled out her foremast and drove on to the North Goodwin Sands where she was wrecked.

### 5. CHEVIOT 1899-1918 Dry cargo steamer

O.N. 97965. 258g, 132n. 130.5 x 21.6 x 9.3 feet.

T.3-cyl. steam engine by North Eastern Marine Engineering Co. Ltd., Wallsend.

*25.4.1891:* Launched by Wood, Skinner & Co., Newcastle upon Tyne (Yard No. 30) for R. Mason, Newcastle upon Tyne. *1899:* Acquired by Christopher Rowbotham. *1908:* Owners became C. Rowbotham & Sons. *1918:* Sold to P. Donovan, Wexford. *1919:* Sold to Munster and Leinster Bank Ltd., Cork. *1924:* Sold to J. Moorhead, Belfast. *1926:* Sold to The North Channel Shipping Co. Ltd. (J. Moorhead, manager), Carnlough, County Antrim. *1929:* Sold to J. Kelly Ltd. (W. Clint, manager), Belfast. *1933:* Broken up at Glasgow.

CHEVIOT                                                                    WSS

HELMSMAN (I)                                              WSS

## 6. HELMSMAN (I) 1903-1923 Dry cargo steamer

O.N. 118279.  458g, 207n.  160.0 x 25.0 x 10.2 feet.

T.3-cyl. steam engine by North Eastern Marine Engineering Co. Ltd., Wallsend.

*22.4.1903:* Launched by Wood, Skinner & Co. Ltd., Newcastle upon Tyne (Yard No. 112) for Christopher Rowbotham. *5.1903:* Completed. *1908:* Owners became C. Rowbotham & Sons. *1923:* Sold to Tyne-Tees Steam Shipping Co. Ltd., Newcastle upon Tyne and renamed CRAGSIDE. *1935:* Renamed CRAG. *1935:* Sold to J.J. King and Co. and broken up at Gateshead.

ARRIVAL on trials                                        WSS

### 7. ARRIVAL 1904-1919 Dry cargo steamer

O.N. 120481. 358g, 126n. 143.0 x 24.1 x 9.2 feet.

T.3-cyl. steam engine by North Eastern Marine Engineering Co. Ltd., Wallsend.

*22.11.1904:* Launched by Wood, Skinner & Co. Ltd., Newcastle upon Tyne (Yard No. 124) for Christopher Rowbotham. *1908:* Owners became C. Rowbotham & Sons. *1919:* Sold to J.J. Stafford, Wexford and renamed ELSIE ANNIE. *1931:* Sold to Wexford Steamship Ltd. (J.J. Stafford, manager), Wexford. *5.2.1936:* Stranded on Wexford Bar while on voyage from Ayr to Wexford with a cargo of coal. Abandoned and sold to F. Bowles and Sons, Cardiff. *19.9.1936:* Refloated and towed to Cardiff but found to be beyond economical repair.

### 8. STEERSMAN (I) 1909-1925 Dry cargo steamer

O.N. 129046. 562g, 254n. 170.2 x 27.5 x 10.7 feet.

T.3-cyl. steam engine by North Eastern Marine Engineering Co. Ltd., Wallsend.

*2.9.1909:* Launched by Wood, Skinner & Co. Ltd., Newcastle upon Tyne (Yard No. 162) for C. Rowbotham & Sons. *29.8.1914-28.9.1914:* On Government service as an ammunition carrier. *29.9.1914-13.3.1919:* On Government service as a store carrier. *1925:* Sold to Continental Lines Ltd., London and renamed CONTINENTAL TRADER. *1927:* Sold to Tyne-Tees Steam Shipping Co. Ltd., Newcastle upon Tyne and renamed LOWICK. *1936:* Sold to Buchan & Hogg (John M. Hogg, manager), Grangemouth and renamed DUNMOIR. *1940:* Sold to Dunmoir Steamship Co. Ltd. (Buchan & Hogg, managers), Grangemouth. *1954:* Sold to Van Heyghen Freres, Belgium. *19.7.1954:* Arrived at Ghent to be broken up.

STEERSMAN (I) WSPL

WHEELSMAN (I)                                                 WSS

### 9. WHEELSMAN (I)  1922-1935  Dry cargo steamer

O.N. 146690.  1394g, 812n.  239.2 x 36.2 x 16.7 feet.

T.3-cyl. steam engine by L. Smit & Zoon Scheeps-en Werktuigbouw, Kinderdijk.

*8.7.1920:* Launched by L. Smit & Zoon Scheeps-en Wertuigbouw, Kinderdijk (Yard No. 796) for their own account as VEERDAM. *1922:* Acquired by C. Rowbotham & Sons and renamed WHEELSMAN. *1935:* Sold to D/S Hetland A/S (T. Basse, manager), Denmark and renamed GUDENAA. *1939:* Sold to Dott. Ing. Cav. Mario Zoboli, Italy and renamed SILVIO SCARONI. *12.6.1941:* Torpedoed and sunk by the British submarine TAKU about 70 miles off Benghazi.

### 10. HELMSMAN (II)  1925-1927

O.N. 122827.  242g, 105n.  120.6 x 21.6 x 9.2 feet.

C.2-cyl. steam engine by Shields Engineering Co. Ltd., North Shields.

*18.7.1905:* Launched by Smith's Dock Co. Ltd., North Shields (Yard No. 773) for James Deuchar, Newcastle upon Tyne as LOCHSIDE. *1925:* Acquired by C. Rowbotham & Sons, fitted with tanks in hold for carrying petroleum by Clelands Graving Dock & Slipway Co. Ltd., Wallsend and renamed HELMSMAN. *27.10.1927:* Sailed from the Medway bound for Stockton with a cargo of petrol. Reported missing presumed foundered in a storm.

### 11. STEERSMAN (II)  1928-1936

O.N. 133021.  594g, 271n.  170.4 x 27.1 x 11.3 feet.

T.3-cyl. steam engine by Bow, McLachlin & Co. Ltd., Paisley.

*29.5.1902:* Launched by Ardrossan Dry Dock & Shipbuilding Co. Ltd., Ardrossan (Yard No. 187) for E. Marcesche & Co., France as ARVOR. *1909:* Renamed ARMORIK. *1912:* Sold to Clydeside Steamship Co. Ltd. (J.B.

HELMSMAN (II)                                                   WSPL

Couper, manager), Glasgow and renamed CLYDEBURN. *1915:* Sold to Keeps
S.S. & Lighterage Co. Ltd. (H. Keep, manager), London. *1916:* Sold to Marga
S.S. Co. Ltd. (C. Angel, manager), Cardiff. *1920:* Sold to A. Andrew & Co. Ltd.,
Cardiff. *1922:* Sold to Iona Shipping Co. Ltd. (J.H. Cubitt & Co., managers),
Newcastle upon Tyne. *1928:* Acquired by C. Rowbotham & Sons, fitted for
the carriage of petroleum in portable tanks and renamed STEERSMAN. *1936:*
Broken up at Stockton on Tees by South Stockton Shipbreaking Co.

STEERSMAN (II)                                                 WSPL

TILLERMAN (I)                                                    WSS

## 12. TILLERMAN (I) 1931-1963

O.N. 162652.   220g, 95n, 230d.   114.5 x 22.1 x 8.2 feet

4-cyl. 4SA Deutz oil engine by Humboldt-Deutzmotoren A.G., Koln-Deutz.

*10.10.1931:* Launched by N.V. Industrieele Maatschappij "De Noord", Alblasserdam (Yard No. 503) for C. Rowbotham & Sons. *1956:* Owners became Bridgeman Shipping Co. Ltd. (C. Rowbotham & Sons (Management) Ltd., managers). *1962:* Renamed TILLERMAN II. *1963:* Sold to shipbreakers in the Netherlands.

RUDDERMAN (I)                                                    WSS

## 13. RUDDERMAN (I) 1934-1967

O.N. 163442. 290g, 130n, 360d. 132.2 x 23.4 x 9.0 feet.

4-cyl. 4SA Deutz oil engine by Humboldt-Deutzmotoren A.G., Koln-Deutz. From *1958:* 5-cyl. 2SA Crossley oil engine by Crossley Brothers Ltd., Manchester.

*27.1.1934:* Launched by N.V. Industrieele Maatschappij "De Noord", Alblasserdam (Yard No. 523) for C. Rowbotham & Sons. 3.*1934:* Completed. 195*6:* Owners became Helmsman Shipping Co. Ltd. (C. Rowbotham & Sons (Management) Ltd., managers). *1958:* Owners became Quarterman Shipping Co. Ltd. (C. Rowbotham & Sons (Management) Ltd., managers). *27.5.1967:* While lying at Ince, prior to loading at Stanlow, an explosion occurred in No. 3 starboard cargo tank. Moved to Ellesmere Port dry dock jetty and found to be completely unseaworthy. *30.6.1967:* After receiving temporary repairs left Ellesmere Port in tow of the tug ALFRED LAMEY for Preston, arriving the same day, to be broken up by T.W. Ward Ltd.

WHEELSMAN (II)                                                          WSPL

## 14. WHEELSMAN (II) 1936-1965

O.N. 164566. 287g, 123n, 355d. 132.2 x 23.4 x 9.0 feet.

6-cyl. 4SA Deutz oil engine by Humboldt-Deutzmotoren A.G., Koln-Deutz.

*4.12.1935:* Launched by N.V. Industrieele Maatschappij "De Noord", Alblasserdam (Yard No. 558) for C. Rowbotham & Sons. *1.1936:* Completed. *1956:* Owners became Bridgeman Shipping Co. Ltd. (C. Rowbotham & Sons (Management) Ltd., managers). *5.4.1965:* Arrived Antwerp, Belgium, to be broken up by Van Den Bossche & Co.

## 15. STEERSMAN (III) 1936-1968

O.N. 164687/L.R. 5339822.  338g, 145n, 414d.  143.3 x 23.7 x 9.3 feet.

6-cyl. 4SA Deutz oil engine by Humboldt-Deutzmotoren A.G., Koln-Deutz. From 4.*1966:* 5-cyl. 2SA Crossley oil engine by Crossley Brothers, Manchester. [Engine made 1951.]  410bhp.  9k.

*16.7.1936:* Launched by N.V. Industrieele Maatschappij "De Noord", Alblasserdam (Yard No. 561) for C. Rowbotham & Sons. *8.1936:* Completed. *1956:* Owners became Steersman Shipping Co. Ltd. (C. Rowbotham & Sons (Management) Ltd., managers). *8.5.1958:* Went aground in fog north of Aberdeen while on passage Immingham to Aberdeen with 380 tons of petrol and gas-oil. *10.5.1958:* Refloated by SALVEDA (782g/43), after discharging part of her cargo into sand dunes, and taken into Aberdeen to discharge balance of cargo before being towed by RIFLEMAN, ex EMPIRE VERA-47 (333g/45) to Hull for repairs. *1963:* Owners became Bridgeman Shipping Co. Ltd. (C. Rowbotham & Sons (Management) Ltd., managers). *1965:* Owners became Quarterman Shipping Co. Ltd. (C. Rowbotham & Sons (Management) Ltd., managers). *1968:* Sold to Scrappingco. S.A., Belgium for breaking up. *29.8.1969:* Demolition commenced at Antwerp.

STEERSMAN (III)                                                    WSPL

GUIDESMAN (I)                                                    WSS

## 16. GUIDESMAN (I) 1938-1965

O.N. 166549.   233g, 92n, 271d.   119.4 x 22.9 x 8.7 feet.

4-cyl. 4SA Deutz oil engine by Humboldt-Deutzmotoren A.G., Koln-Deutz. From *2.1960:* 4-cyl. 2SA Crossley oil engine by Crossley Brothers Ltd., Manchester.

*5.7.1938:* Launched by N.V. Industrieele Maatschappij "De Noord", Alblasserdam (Yard No. 571) for C. Rowbotham & Sons. *8.1938:* Completed. *1956:* Owners became Steersman Shipping Co. Ltd. (C. Rowbotham & Sons (Management) Ltd., managers). *1963:* Owners became Helmsman Shipping Co. Ltd. (C. Rowbotham & Sons (Management) Ltd., managers). *1964:* Renamed GUIDESMAN II. *6.1.1965:* Arrived Bo'ness to be broken up by P. & W. MacLellan Ltd.

GUIDESMAN (I)                                                    WSS

## 17. CHARTSMAN (I) 1946-1966

O.N. 169730/L.R. 5069063.  340g, 135n, 421d.  146.8 x 23.7 x 9.3 feet.
From *1966*: 330g, 146n, 274d.

4-cyl. 2SA British Auxiliaries oil engine by British Auxiliaries Ltd., Glasgow. 395bhp. 9k.

*14.10.1943:* Launched by Rowhedge Ironworks Co. Ltd., Rowhedge (Yard No. 629) for the Ministry of War Transport (C. Rowbotham & Sons, managers), London as EMPIRE BOXER. *12.2.1944:* Completed. *12.2.1944-17.4.1946:* In use as a tanker in coastal and short sea trade. *1946:* Acquired by C. Rowbotham & Sons and renamed CHARTSMAN. *1956:* Owners became Steersman Shipping Co. Ltd. (C. Rowbotham & Sons (Management) Ltd., managers). *1963:* Owners became Quarterman Shipping Co. Ltd. (C. Rowbotham & Sons (Management) Ltd., managers). *1.1966:* Sold to Coastal Prospecting Ltd. [Union Corporation, South Africa] (Ashmead (Padstow) Ltd., Padstow, managers), London and renamed  BAYMEAD. *6.1966:* Converted to a suction dredger/tin recovery vessel by N. Holman & Sons Ltd., Penzance. *12.1968:* Sold to Pounds Shipowners & Shipbreakers Ltd., Tipnor, Portsmouth. *9.1969:* Sold to T.J. Bowen & P.D. Caines, Southampton. *1974:* Sold to T. Holden, Northam, Southampton for breaking up.

CHARTSMAN (I) at Jersey                                    Dave Hocquard

## 18. HELMSMAN (III) 1948-1970

O.N. 165674/L.R. 5147293.  493g, 181n, 586d.  168.2 x 25.9 x 9.8 feet.
From *4.1962:* 531g, 209n, 836d.  175' 6" x 25' 11" x 12' 4 ".

8-cyl. 4SA Deutz oil engine by Humboldt-Deutzmotoren A.G., Koln-Deutz. From *4.1962:* 8-cyl. 2SA Brons oil engine by Drypool Engineering & Drydock Co. Ltd., Hull.  600bhp.

*21.11.1936:* Launched by N.V. Scheepsbouwwerf v/h De Groot & Van Vliet, Slikkerveer (Yard No. 212) for N.V. Tankreederij OBO (Nederlandsch Bevrachtingskantoor N.V., managers), Netherlands as OBOR. *1.1937:* Completed. *1937:* Sold to Harker (Coasters) Ltd. (J. Harker Ltd., managers), Knottingley and renamed BEDALE H. *1948:* Acquired by C. Rowbotham & Sons and renamed HELMSMAN. *1956:* Owners became Helmsman Shipping

HELMSMAN (III) at Jersey as built                    Dave Hocquard

Co. Ltd. (C. Rowbotham & Sons (Management) Ltd., managers). *4.1962:*
Rebuilt and re-engined by Drypool Engineering & Drydock Co. Ltd., Hull.
*4.1970:* Sold to Van Den Bossche & Co., Belgium for breaking up. *1.6.1970:*
Demolition commenced at Antwerp.

HELMSMAN (III) as rebuilt                              WSS

### 19. BRIDGEMAN (I) 1950-1969

O.N. 183242/L.R. 5051793.  369g, 144n, 504d.  153' 6" x 25' 7" x 10' 4".

7-cyl. 2SA Deutz oil engine by Humboldt-Deutzmotoren A.G., Koln-Deutz. From *1960:* 5-cyl. 2SA Crossley oil engine by Crossley Brothers Ltd., Manchester. [Engine made *1952.*]  8,5k.

*4.11.1938:* Launched by N.V. Industrieele Maatschappij De Noord, Alblasserdam (Yard No. 575) for Skibsaksjeselskap Tripp (Oswald Aamodt, manager), Norway as TRIPP. *1939:* Completed. *1950:* Acquired by C. Rowbotham & Sons and renamed BRIDGEMAN. *1956:* Owners became Bridgeman Shipping Co. Ltd. (C. Rowbotham & Sons (Management) Ltd., managers). *1965:* Owners became Quarterman Shipping Co. Ltd. (C. Rowbotham & Sons (Management) Ltd., managers). *1969:* Sold to Marine Disposals Ltd., Preesall, Nr. Blackpool, Lancashire and renamed MARINE SEAWAY. *1973:* Sold to Effluents Services Ltd., Macclesfield. *2.1981:* Sold to Pemberton & Carlyon for breaking up at Garston.

BRIDGEMAN (I) at Jersey on 14th March 1958                Dave Hocquard

### 20. LEADSMAN (I) 1951-1962

O.N. 180265/L.R. 6513621.  396g, 206n, 414d.  148' 2" x 27' 0" x 10' 0".

4-cyl. 2SA Crossley oil engine by Crossley Brothers Ltd., Manchester.

*5.1944:* Launched by Henry Scarr Ltd., Hessle (Yard No. 445) for the Ministry of War Transport (C. Rowbotham & Sons, managers), London as CHANT 11. *5.7.1944:* Completed. *5.7.1944-19.6.1946:* In use as a tanker. *1945:* Transferred to the Admiralty for naval duties. *1.4.1946:* Owners became the Ministry of Transport, London. *1946:* Sold to T.B. McEwen, resold to Société Nord Africaine d'Armement (Van Castricum & Co. Ltd., managers), Morocco and renamed PINARD. *1951:* Acquired by Helmsman Shipping Co. Ltd. (C. Rowbotham & Sons, managers) and renamed LEADSMAN. *1956:* Owners became Quarterman Shipping Co. Ltd. (C. Rowbotham & Sons (Management) Ltd., managers). *1962:* Sold to Pounds Shipowners and Shipbreakers Ltd., Tipnor, Portsmouth. *1965:* Sold to S. Bezzina & Sons Ltd., Malta. *1968:* Renamed UADDAN. *1974:* Broken up in Spain.

LEADSMAN (I)                                                          WSS

## 21. QUARTERMAN (I) 1953-1970

O.N. 185947/L.R. 5287782.   470g, 190n, 584d.   179' 4" x 27' 9" x 10' 3".

5-cyl. 2SA Polar oil engine by British Polar Engines Ltd., Glasgow. 450bhp. 9k.

*9.7.1953:* Launched by Clelands (Successors) Ltd., Wallsend (Yard No. 183) for Helmsman Shipping Co. Ltd. (C. Rowbotham & Sons, managers). *9.1953:* Completed. *1956:* Owners became Quarterman Shipping Co. Ltd. (C. Rowbotham & Sons (Management) Ltd., managers). *1965:* Owners became Helmsman Shipping Co. Ltd. (C. Rowbotham & Sons (Management) Ltd., managers). *1970:* Sold to Ioannis Daifas, Piraeus, Greece and renamed MEGALOCHARI II. *1984:* Sold to Christos Sidereas & Co., Piraeus, Greece. *1986:* Sold to J. Daifas & Co., Piraeus, Greece. *1986:* Broken up in Greece.

QUARTERMAN (I)                                                       WSS

49

POINTSMAN (I) on the river Mersey in September 1966     Dave Hocquard

## 22. POINTSMAN (I)  1956-1968

O.N. 163454/L.R. 528044.  1174g, 574n.  233' 0" x 35' 1" x 14' 11 ".
T.3-cyl. steam engine by D. Rowan & Co. Ltd., Glasgow.  10k.
*28.2.1934:* Launched by Blythswood Shipbuilding Co. Ltd., Glasgow (Yard No. 36) for Hadley Shipping Co. Ltd., London as BASSETHOUND. *4.1934:* Completed. *1954:* Sold to Thames Welding Co. Ltd., London. *1956:* Acquired by Helmsman Shipping Co. Ltd. (C. Rowbotham & Sons (Management) Ltd., managers) and renamed POINTSMAN. *1968:* Sold to Scrappingco S.A. for breaking up at Willebroek, Belgium. *10.1968:* Demolition commenced.

OARSMAN (I)                                Andrew Huckett Collection

## 23. OARSMAN (I) 1959-1973

O.N. 300822/L.R. 5259840. 778g, 341n, 1000d. 203' 6" x 30' 10" x 12' 6".

8-cyl. 2SA Crossley oil engine by Crossley Brothers Ltd., Manchester. 875bhp. 10k.

*25.8.1958:* Launched by Drypool Engineering & Drydock Co. Ltd., Hull (Yard No. 1) for Quarterman Shipping Co. Ltd. (C. Rowbotham & Sons (Management) Ltd., managers). *1.1959:* Completed. *1965:* Owners became Helmsman Shipping Co. Ltd. (C. Rowbotham & Sons (Management) Ltd., managers). *1972:* Owners became C. Rowbotham & Sons (Management) Ltd. *4.1973:* Sold to Normandie Dredging & Shipping Co. Ltd., Bitterne, Southampton and renamed SOLENT LEE. *7-12.1973:* Converted into a suction dredger/sand carrier. *12.1974:* Sold to Lee Shipping Ltd. (Normandie Dredging & Shipping Co. Ltd., managers), Eastleigh, Hampshire. *1976:* Sold to Redland Purle Ltd., Rayleigh, Essex. *2.1979:* Sold to Lee Shipping Ltd., Eastleigh, Hampshire. *1980:* Sold to Solent Aggregates Ltd., Southampton. *1989:* Broken up by Tollgate Medway Ltd., Rainham, Kent.

ANCHORMAN (I)                                           WSS

## 24. ANCHORMAN (I) 1962-1983

O.N. 302880/L.R. 5016016. 795g, 383n, 1172d. 203' 0" x 30' 9" x 12' 9 ".

12-cyl. 2SA Brons vee oil engine by Drypool Engineering & Drydock Co. Ltd., Hull. 900bhp. 10k.

*14.12.1961:* Launched by Drypool Engineering & Drydock Co. Ltd., Hull (Yard No. 4) for Helmsman Shipping Co. Ltd. (C. Rowbotham & Sons (Management) Ltd., managers). *1.1962:* Completed. *1972:* Owners became C. Rowbotham & Sons (Management) Ltd. *1981:* Owners became Rowbotham Tankships Ltd. *1983:* Sold to M. Koutlakis & H. & P. Leonardos, Piraeus, Greece and renamed VASILIKI III. *1984:* Sold to Vasiliki III Shipping Co. (Vasilios Shipping Co., Piraeus, agents), Piraeus, Greece. *1993:* Sold to Storel Shipping Co., Honduras and renamed GREMON. At unknown date laid up and under arrest at Durres, Albania. *3.1997:* Hijacked by rioters and stranded owing to engine problems. Previous to *1.6.1997:* Refloated and moved to Golem beach and adandoned.

TILLERMAN (II) anchored Bouley Bay, Jersey on 16th November 1969
Dave Hocquard

## 25. TILLERMAN (II) 1963-1986

O.N. 304431/L.R. 5409433.   807g, 387n, 1172d.   203' 0" x 30' 9" x 12' 9 ".

12-cyl. 2SA Brons vee oil engine by Drypool Engineering & Drydock Co. Ltd., Hull. 900bhp. 10k.

*7.1.1963:* Launched by Drypool Engineering & Drydock Co. Ltd., Hull (Yard No. 5) for Bridgeman Shipping Co. Ltd. (C. Rowbotham & Sons (Management) Ltd., managers). *1.1963:* Completed. *1965:* Owners became Helmsman Shipping Co. Ltd. (C. Rowbotham & Sons (Management) Ltd., managers). *1972:* Owners became C. Rowbotham & Sons (Management) Ltd. *1981:* Owners became Rowbotham Tankships Ltd. *1986:* Sold to Luvia Investment Ltd., Gibraltar then International Trading & Supply Co. Ltd.,

TILLERMAN (II)                                                                    WSS

Jeddah, Saudi Arabia and renamed OHOUD. *1987:* Sold to Caribene Investments Ltd. (Blue Seas Overseas S.A., Athens, managers), St. Vincent and the Grenadines and renamed AL AMIN. *1990:* Sold to Luvia Investments Ltd., Gibraltar and renamed FLYING TRADER, with registry transferred to Honduras. *1991:* Sold to Orri United Lines Co. Ltd., Jeddah, Saudi Arabia and renamed AL MAHROUKAT AL AWAL. *1992:* Sold to International Bunkering Co. Ltd., Jeddah, Saudi Arabia. *1997:* Renamed AL-ZAHRA. *8.5.1997-7.5.1998:* Registry temporarily transferred to Belize. *1999:* Sold to Abdulelah Jaffar Hadi & A Abdusalam Faisal Mohammad, Saudi Arabia and renamed FAISAL IV. Still in service.

GUIDESMAN (II)                                              WSPL

## 26. GUIDESMAN (II) 1964-1983

O.N. 306183/L.R. 6421866. 799g, 379n, 1172d. 203' 0" x 30' 0" x 12' 9 ".

12-cyl. 2SA Brons vee oil engine by Drypool Engineering & Drydock Co. Ltd., Hull. 950bhp. 10k.

*16.9.1964:* Launched by Drypool Engineering & Drydock Co. Ltd., Hull (Yard No. 12) for Helmsman Shipping Co. Ltd. (C. Rowbotham & Sons (Management) Ltd., managers). *11.1964:* Completed. *1972:* Owners became C. Rowbotham & Sons (Management) Ltd. *1981:* Owners became Rowbotham & Sons Tankships Ltd. *1983:* Sold to M. Koutlakis & H. & P. Leonardos, Piraeus, Greece and renamed VASILIKI IV. *1984:* Sold to Vasiliki IV Shipping Co. (Vasilios Shipping Co., Piraeus, agents), Piraeus, Greece. *1987:* Sold to Maritima Canopus S.A., Caracas, Venezuela and renamed BIANCA MARIE. *17.11.1987:* Sustained main engine damage at Curacao. *12.1987:* Left Curacao in tow for Puerto Cabello. Later abandoned as a hulk on an unknown beach.

## 27. CHARTSMAN (II) 1967-1983

O.N. 309913/L.R. 6709608. 787g, 367n, 1172d. 203' 0" x 30' 10" x 12' 9".

12-cyl. 2SA Brons vee oil engine by Drypool Engineering & Drydock Co. Ltd., Hull. 950bhp. 10k.

*6.2.1967:* Launched by Drypool Engineering & Drydock Co. Ltd., Hull (Yard No. 21) for Helmsman Shipping Co. Ltd. (C. Rowbotham & Sons (Management) Ltd., managers). *5.1967:* Completed. *1972:* Owners became C. Rowbotham & Sons (Management) Ltd. *1976:* Renamed RIVER LEE. *1981:* Owners became Rowbotham Tankships Ltd. *1983:* Sold to Inter Latex Compania Naviera S.A. (Andres Perdomo S.L., Las Palmas de Gran Canaria, Canary Islands, agents), Panama and renamed UCANCA. *1993:* Sold to Arendale Overseas S.A., Panama. *1994:* Renamed PALMAR 1. *1.1994:* Sold to Canary Tanker Corporation, Belize and renamed ROMANA. Still in service.

CHARTSMAN (II)                                                                WSS

## 28. WHEELSMAN (III) 1967-1992

O.N. 309946/L.R. 6712447. 2897g, 1536n, 4574d. 322' 6" x 47' 3" x 19' 11 ".

9-cyl. 4SA Ruston oil engine by Ruston & Hornsby Ltd., Lincoln. 2380bhp. 12kn.

*29.3.1967:* Launched by Clelands Shipbuilding Co. Ltd., Wallsend (Yard No. 293) for C. Rowbotham & Sons (Management) Ltd. *5.1967:* Completed. *1981:* Owners became Ingram Overseas Inc. (Rowbotham Tankships Ltd., managers). *1985:* Owners became Rowbotham Tankships Ltd. *1987:* Registry transferred to the Isle of Man. *1992:* Owners became Rowbotham Tankships (Gibraltar) Ltd. (Rowbotham Tankships Ltd., managers), Gibraltar. *9.1992:* Sold to Tomani Shipping Co. Ltd. (N.J. Pateras S.A., Carouge, Switzerland, managers), Gibraltar and to be renamed ELSMAN. *1992:* Sold to Petro-Med Oils (Nigeria) Ltd., Apapa, Nigeria and renamed ALIDA. *1993:* Renamed POWE. Still in service.

WHEELSMAN (III)                                                    WSS

## 29. LEADSMAN (II)  1968-1985

O.N. 336922/L.R. 6818526.   843g, 406n, 1469d.   205' 0" x 32' 9" x 13' 9".
From *1985:* 836g, 405n, 1493d.   61,63 x 9,99 x 4,192 metres.

12-cyl. 2SA Brons vee oil engine by Drypool Engineering & Drydock Co. Ltd.,
Hull.  1120bhp.  11k.

*11.6.1968:* Launched by Drypool Engineering & Drydock Co. Ltd., Hull (Yard
No. 23) for Helmsman Shipping Co. Ltd. (C. Rowbotham & Sons
(Management) Ltd., managers). *10.1968:* Completed. *1972:* Owners became
C. Rowbotham & Sons (Management) Ltd. *1981:* Owners became Ingram
International Ltd. (Rowbotham Tankships Ltd., managers). *6.1985:* Sold to
Effluents Services Ltd., Macclesfield,  converted to an effluent carrier,
shortened and renamed ALSTON. *1996:* Sold to Pounds Marine Shipping
Ltd., Portchester, Fareham. *4.1997:* Sold to Hydria I Maritime (Hidrodotiki
Group of Companies, managers), Piraeus, Greece and renamed ALS. *1998:*
Renamed IRINI. Still in service.

LEADSMAN (II) at Jersey on 7th December 1975          Dave Hocquard

RUDDERMAN (II)                                                    WSS

## 30. RUDDERMAN (II) 1968-1986

O.N. 336939/L.R. 6818552. 1592g, 926n, 2957d. 274' 0" x 41' 4" x 16' 10".

16-cyl. 2SA Brons vee oil engine by Drypool Engineering & Drydock Co. Ltd., Hull. 1500bhp. 12k.

*12.6.1968:* Launched by Cochrane & Sons Ltd., Selby (Yard No. 1519) for Helmsman Shipping Co. Ltd. (C. Rowbotham & Sons (Management) Ltd., managers). *11.1968:* Completed. *1972:* Owners became C. Rowbotham & Sons (Management) Ltd. *1981:* Owners became Ingram Overseas Ltd. (Rowbotham Tankships Ltd., managers). *1985:* Owners became Rowbotham Tankships Ltd. *1986:* Sold to Soconav Inc., Montreal, Canada and renamed HENRI TELLIER. *1993:* Managers became QMT Navigation Inc., Montreal, Canada. *1995:* Managers became Caribbean Seabridge Ltd., Port of Spain,, registry transferred to Trinidad & Tobago and renamed RAMA J. *1996:* Converted to a water tanker. *1997:* Sold to Epxon Oil Producing Co. Ltd., Apapa, Nigeria and renamed CHRISTINE. Still in service.

POINTSMAN (II) at Harwich                              Bernard McCall

### 31. POINTSMAN (II) 1970-1992

O.N. 339358/L.R. 7018410. 2886g, 1530n, 4620d. 325' 9" x 47' 3" x 20' 2".

9-cyl. 4SA Ruston oil engine by English Electric Diesels Ltd., Ruston Engine Division, Lincoln. 2460bhp. 12k.

*6.5.1970:* Launched by Goole Shipbuilding & Repairing Co. Ltd., Goole (Yard No. 568) for Helmsman Shipping Co. Ltd. (C. Rowbotham & Sons (Management) Ltd., managers). *9.1970:* Completed. *1972:* Owners became C. Rowbotham & Sons (Management) Ltd. *1981:* Owners became Ingram Overseas Corporation (Rowbotham Tankships Ltd., managers). *15.6.1984:* Suffered a series of explosions in her pump room while lying at Milford Haven. Four people were killed. *1985:* Owners became Rowbotham Tankships Ltd. *1.1992:* Sold to Sandown Shipping (Petromarine S.A., Bordeaux, managers), France. *4.1992:* Delivered and renamed MA BRO. *1994:* Sold to Donadiem Shipping Ltd. (Petromarine S.A., Bordeaux, managers), St. Vincent and the Grenadines. *1995:* Renamed ARGUIN. *2000:* Sold to unspecified owners, St. Vincent and the Grenadines and renamed MAGDA. Still in service.

STEERSMAN (IV)                                                             WSS

### 32. STEERSMAN (IV) 1970-1992

O.N. 341182/L.R. 7026431. 1567g, 953n, 2932d. 274' 0" x 41' 4" x 16' 10".

16-cyl. 2SA Brons vee oil engine by Appingedammer Brons, Appingedam. 1860bhp. 12k.

*21.7.1970:* Launched by Cochrane & Sons Ltd., Selby (Yard No. 1533) for Helmsman Shipping Co. Ltd. (C. Rowbotham & Sons (Management) Ltd., managers). *12.1970:* Completed. *1972:* Owners became C. Rowbotham & Sons (Management) Ltd. *1976:* Renamed RIVER SHANNON. *1981:* Owners became Rowbotham Tankships Ltd. *1987:* Registry transferred to the Isle of Man. *1992:* Owners became Rowbotham Tankships (Gibraltar) Ltd. (Rowbotham Tankships Ltd., managers), Gibraltar. *12.1992:* Sold to Skopelos Shipping Co. Ltd., Piraeus, Greece. *2.1993:* Delivered and renamed SKOPELOS. *1997:* Sold to Al Faihaa Trading L.L.C., Dubai, United Arab Emirates and renamed AL BATOOL. *1998:* sold to Kamel H. Mohamed, Belize. Still in service.

HELMSMAN (IV) being launched on 5th November 1971                    WSPL

### 33. HELMSMAN (IV) 1972-1993

O.N. 343160/L.R. 7123370. 3705g, 2308n, 6165d.   341' 0" x 49' 1" x 23' 0".

16-cyl. 4SA Ruston vee oil engine by Ruston Paxman Diesels Ltd., Newton-le-Willows. 3520bhp. 13k.

*5.11.1971:* Launched by Cochrane & Sons Ltd., Selby (Yard No. 1540) for Helmsman Shipping Co. Ltd. (C. Rowbotham & Sons (Management) Ltd., managers). *4.1972:* Completed. *1972:* Owners became C. Rowbotham & Sons (Management) Ltd. *1981:* Owners became Rowbotham Tankships Ltd. *1987:* Registry transferred to the Isle of Man. *1992:* Owners became

HELMSMAN (IV)                                                         WSS

Rowbotham Tankships (Gibraltar) Ltd. (Rowbotham Tankships Ltd., managers), Gibraltar. *1.2.1993:* Owners became P&O Tankships (Gibraltar) Ltd. (P&O Tankships Ltd., managers), Gibraltar. *3.1994:* Sold to Galana Petroleum Ltd. (Galana Marine Ltd., St. Helier, Jersey, managers), Mombasa, Kenya and renamed RUFIJI with Gibraltar flag retained. *1997:* Sold to Seagull Maritime Ltd. (Alba Petroleum Ltd., Mombasa, managers), Bahamas and renamed SEAGULL. Still in service.

BRIDGEMAN (II) at Plymouth on 5th July 1974          Ambrose Greenway

### 34. BRIDGEMAN (II) 1972-1993

O.N. 358466/L.R. 7210812.   3701g, 2308n, 6210d.   340' 0" x 49' 1" x 2' 11".

16-cyl. 4SA Ruston vee oil engine by Ruston Paxman Diesels Ltd., Colchester. 3520bhp.   13k.

*11.4.1972:* Launched by Hall, Russell & Co. Ltd., Aberdeen (Yard No. 955) for Helmsman Shipping Co. Ltd. (C. Rowbotham & Sons (Management) Ltd., managers). *6.1972:* Completed. *1972:* Owners became C. Rowbotham & Sons (Management) Ltd. *1981:* Owners became Rowbotham Tankships Ltd. *1987:* Registry transferred to the Isle of Man. *1992:* Owners became Rowbotham Tankships (Gibraltar) Ltd. (Rowbotham Tankships Ltd., managers). *1.2.1993:* Owners became P&O Tankships (Gibraltar) Ltd. (P&O Tankships Ltd., managers), Gibraltar. *3.1994:* Sold to Pollux Ltd. (Apina Ship Management ApS, Naestved, Denmark, managers), St. Vincent and the Grenadines and renamed SANDY. *1995:* Sold to Petrostar Co. Ltd., Jeddah, Saudi Arabia and renamed NEJMAT EL PETROL XXV. *1998:* Sold to Perseverance Marine Corporation (Norbulk Shipping UK Ltd., Glasgow, managers), Bahamas. *1999:* Managers become Global Reefer Trading Ltd., Togham, Farnham. Still in service.

### 35. ASTRAMAN 1973-1993

O.N. 358853/L.R. 7229306. 1599g, 1079n, 3202d. 286' 9" x 45' 1" x 18' 0".

2 8-cyl. 4SA Ruston vee oil engines by Ruston Paxman Diesels Ltd., Newton-le-Willows. 3520bhp. 14k.

*26.9.1972:* Launched by Cochrane & Sons Ltd., Selby (Yard No. 1543) for Helmsman Shipping Co. Ltd. (C. Rowbotham & Sons (Management) Ltd., managers). *3.1973:* Completed. *1973:* Owners became C. Rowbotham & Sons (Management) Ltd. *1981:* Owners became Rowbotham Tankships Ltd. *1987:* Registry transferred to the Isle of Man. *1992:* Owners became Rowbotham Tankships (Hong Kong) Ltd. (Rowbotham Tankships Ltd., managers), Hong Kong. *1.2.1993:* Owners became P&O Tankships (Hong Kong) Ltd. (P&O Tankships Ltd., managers), Hong Kong. *6.1995:* Sold to Pacific Dynamic Ltd. (Alva Investments Corporation, London, managers), Hong Kong and renamed STRAMAN. *1995:* Sold to Ihlas Finans Kurumu S.A. (Ferman Denizcilik ve Ticaret A.S. (Ferman Shipping & Trade Inc.), Istanbul, managers), Istanbul, Turkey and renamed FERMAN 1. *1999:* Sold to EuroOil Ltd., Bolivia and renamed ARABIAN QUEEN. *2001:* Flag transferred to Georgia, *2001:* Sold to Indian shipbreakers. *12.2.2001:* Arrived Mumbai to be broken up.

ASTRAMAN                                                                    WSPL

### 36. QUARTERMAN II 1973-1992

O.N. 360535/L.R. 7304388. 1226g, 761n, 2050d. 239' 0" x 35' 5" x 16' 1".

8-cyl. 4SA Ruston vee oil engine by Ruston Paxman Diesels Ltd., Newton-le-Willows. 1460bhp. 11k.

*18.1.1973:* Launched by R. Dunston (Hessle) Ltd., Hessle (Yard No. S891) for C. Rowbotham & Sons (Managament) Ltd. *6.1973:* Completed. *1981:* Owners became Ingram Overseas Ltd. (Rowbotham Tankships Ltd., managers). *1985:* Owners became Rowbotham Tankships Ltd. *1987:* Registry transferred to the Isle of Man. *1.1992:* Sold to Bulk Oil Tanzania, Dar es Salaam, Tanzania and renamed DK II, with registry transferred to St. Vincent and the Grenadines. *9.1992:* Sold to Rapid Investments Ltd. (Bulk Oil Tanzania Ltd., Dar es Salaam, managers) Tortola, British Virgin Islands, with St. Vincent and the Grenadines registry retained. *1993:* Registry transferred to Tanzania. *1994:* Registry transferred to St. Vincent and the Grenadines. *1995:* Registry transferred to Tanzania. Still in service.

QUARTERMAN (II) passing Penarth Head          Bernard McCall


### 37. POLARISMAN 1973-1993

O.N. 360752/L.R. 7304390. 1596g, 1079n, 3151d.   286' 9" x 45' 1" x 17' 11".
2 8-cyl. 4SA Ruston vee oil engines by Ruston Paxman Diesels Ltd., Newton-le-Willows.   3520bhp.   14k.

*19.1.1973:* Launched by Cochrane & Sons Ltd., Selby (Yard No. 1544) for C. Rowbotham & Sons (Management) Ltd. *8.1973:* Completed. *1981:* Owners became Rowbotham Tankships Ltd. *1987:* Registry transferred to the Isle of Man. *1992:* Owners became Rowbotham Tankships (Gibraltar) Ltd. (Rowbotham Tankships Ltd., managers), Gibraltar. *1.2.1993:* Owners became P&O Tankships (Gibraltar) Ltd. (P&O Tankships Ltd., managers), Gibraltar. *7.1994:* Sold to Milbank Ltd. (Jaisu Shipping Co. Private Ltd., Kandla, India, managers), Gibraltar and renamed GOD PRESTIGE, with registry transferred to St. Vincent and the Grenadines. Still in service.

POLARISMAN                                           WSPL

ORIONMAN                                    J.K. Byass

## 38. ORIONMAN  1975-1993

O.N. 363714/L.R. 7340966.   3623g, 2194n, 6176d.

103,64 x 14,97 x 7,100 metres.

16-cyl. 4SA Ruston vee oil engine by Ruston Paxman Diesels Ltd., Newton-le-Willows. 3520bhp.   13k.

*14.1.1975:* Launched by Hall, Russell & Co. Ltd., Aberdeen (Yard No. 964) for C. Rowbotham & Sons (Management) Ltd. *5.1975:* Completed. *1981:* Owners became Rowbotham Tankships Ltd. *1987:* Converted from a chemical tanker into a clean oil tanker and registry transferred to the Isle of Man. *1992:* Owners became Rowbotham Tankships (Hong Kong) Ltd. (Rowbotham Tankships Ltd., managers), Hong Kong.   *1.2.1993:* Owners became P&O Tankships (Hong Kong) Ltd. (P&O Tankships Ltd., managers), Hong Kong. *1994:* Sold to SCAN S.r.l., Buenos Aires, Argentina and renamed SCANNER 1. *1997:* Registry transferred to Panama. *1998:* Registry transferred to Argentina. *1999:* Owners became Naviera Scan S.A. and registery transferred to Panama. Still in service.

ORIONMAN at Eastham                          Bernard McCall

CENTAURMAN at Eastham                                    Bernard McCall

## 39. CENTAURMAN 1976-1987

O.N. 366040/L.R. 7427142.   2475g, 1112n, 3560d.
89,18 x 14,03 x 5,900 metres.

6-cyl. 4SA Mirrlees oil engine by Mirrlees Blackstone (Stockport) Ltd.,
Stockport. 3600bhp. 13,5k.

*26.9.1975:* Launched by Hall, Russell & Co. Ltd., Aberdeen (Yard No. 969) for
C. Rowbotham & Sons (Management) Ltd. *1.1976:* Completed. *1981:* Owners
became Rowbotham Tankships Ltd. *1983:* Renamed ESSEX TROPHY. *1983:*
Renamed CENTAURMAN. *1987:* Sold to Lometa Ltd. (Buries Markes (Ship
Management) Ltd., London, managers), Hong Kong and renamed
MAPLEWOOD. *1989:* Sold to Stolt Maplewood Inc. (Stolt-Nielsens Rederi
A/S, Haugesund, managers), Norway (NIS) and renamed STOLT MAPLE-
WOOD. *1996:* Sold to Derby Shipping Ltd. (Vita Marine S.A.M., Monte Carlo,
Monaco, managers), St. Vincent and the Grenadines and renamed
MAPLEWOOD. *1998:* Managers became Monte Carlo Maritime Services,
Monte Carlo, Monaco. *2000:* Sold to Gulf Tankers S.A. (Birlesik Denizcilik ve
Armatorluk Sanayii Ticaret A.S. (Birlesik Shipping), Istanbul, Turkey,
managers), St. Vincent and the Grenadines and renamed MAPLE. Still in service.

ESSEX TROPHY, ex Centaurman at Hull                        Bill Harvey

### 40. STELLAMAN (I) 1976-1987

O.N. 366045/L.R. 7342275. 1513g, 835n, 2324d.
79,51 x 13,54 x 5,265 metres.

16-cyl. 4SA Allen vee oil engine by W.H. Allen, Sons & Co. Ltd., Bedford.
2680bhp. 13,75k.

*27.3.1975:* Launched by Cochrane Shipbuilders Ltd., Selby (Yard No. 1560)
for Ingram Ocean Carriers Ltd. (C. Rowbotham & Sons (Management) Ltd.,
managers). *2.1976:* Completed. *1976:* Owners became Transnational
Insurance Ltd (C. Rowbotham & Sons (Management) Ltd., managers). *1979:*
Owners became C. Rowbotham & Sons (Management) Ltd. *1981:* Owners
became Rowbotham Tankships Ltd. *1987:* Sold to Lenitz Ltd. (Buries Markes
(Ship Management) Ltd., London, managers), Hong Kong and renamed
CEDARWOOD. *1989:* Sold to Stolt Cedarwood Inc. (Stolt-Nielsens Rederi A/S,
Haugesund, managers), Norway (NIS) and renamed STOLT CEDARWOOD.
*1990:* Registry transferred to Liberia. *1995:* Sold to TRANS KA Tankers
Management Co. Ltd. (TRANS KA Tanker Isletmeciligi Ticaret Ltd. Sirketi),
Istanbul, Turkey and renamed KEREM KA. Still in service.

STELLAMAN (I)                                                              WSS

### 41. VEGAMAN 1976-1987

O.N. 366184/L.R. 7427154. 2475g, 1112n, 3575d.
89,18 x 14,03 x 5,900 metres.

6-cyl. 4SA Mirrlees oil engine by Mirrlees Blackstone (Stockport) Ltd.,
Stockport. 3600bhp. 13,5k.

*15.1.1976:* Launched by Hall, Russell & Co. Ltd., Aberdeen (Yard No. 970) for
C. Rowbotham & Sons (Management) Ltd. *6.1976:* Completed. *1981:* Owners
became Rowbotham Tankships Ltd. *1983:* Renamed ESSEX TRIUMPH. *1983:*
Renamed VEGAMAN. *1987:* Sold to Pasado Ltd. (Buries Markes (Ship
Management) Ltd., London, managers), Hong Kong and renamed
OAKWOOD. *1989:* Sold to Stolt Oakwood Inc. (Stolt-Nielsens Rederi A/S,
Haugesund, managers), Norway (NIS) and renamed STOLT OAKWOOD.
*1996:* Sold to Cecilia Maritime S.A. (Naviera Alvargonzalez S.A., Gijon,
Spain, managers), Panama and renamed ARAMO. Still in service.

VEGAMAN                                                          WSS

## 42. MARSMAN 1976-1987

O.N. 366284/L.R. 7392256. 1513g, 835n, 2324d.
79,51 x 13,54 x 5,265 metres.

16-cyl. 4SA Allen vee oil engine by W.H. Allen, Sons & Co. Ltd., Bedford.
2680bhp. 13,75k.

*22.8.1975:* Launched by Cochrane & Sons Ltd., Selby (Yard No. 1561) for
Transnational Insurance Ltd. (C. Rowbotham & Sons (Management) Ltd.,
managers). *9.1976:* Completed. *1979:* Owners became C. Rowbotham &
Sons (Management) Ltd. *1981:* Owners became Rowbotham Tankships Ltd.
*1987:* Sold to Rimini Ltd. (Buries Markes (Ship Management) Ltd., London,
managers), Hong Kong and renamed BIRCHWOOD. *1989:* Sold to Stolt
Birchwood Inc. (Stolt-Nielsens Rederi A/S, Haugesund, managers), Norway
(NIS) and renamed STOLT BIRCHWOOD. *1994:* Sold to Karimata Investments
Corporation (P.T. Submare Laboro, Jakarta, Indonesia, managers), Panana
and renamed OCEEANA KAREEMATA. Still in service.

MARSMAN on the river Tyne                            Nigel J. Cutts

65

OARSMAN (II)                                                    WSS

## 43. OARSMAN (II) 1980-1993

O.N. 388272/L.R. 7816850.    1550g, 961n, 2547d.
76,13 x 12,53 x 4,861 metres.

8-cyl. 4SA Ruston vee oil engine by Ruston Diesels Ltd., Newton-le-Willows.
1880bhp.    10,5k.

*18.10.1979:* Launched by R. Dunston (Hessle) Ltd., Hessle (Yard No. 921) for
C. Rowbotham & Sons (Management) Ltd. *1.1980:* Completed. *1981:* Owners
became Rowbotham Tankships Ltd. *1987:* Registry transferred to the Isle of
Man. *1992:* Owners became Rowbotham Tankships (Gibraltar) Ltd.
(Rowbotham Tankships Ltd., managers), Gibraltar. *1.2.1993:* Owners became
P&O Tankships (Gibraltar) Ltd. (P&O Tankships Ltd., managers), Gibraltar.
*30.12.1996:* P&O Tankships Ltd. acquired by James Fisher & Sons Public
Limited Company and vessel transferred to the ownership of James Fisher
(Gibraltar) Ltd. (James Fisher Tankships Ltd., managers), retaining Gibraltar
registry. *1999:* Managers became James Fisher (Shipping Services) Ltd. Still
in service.

CABLEMAN passing Penarth Head on 23rd June 1987        Bernard McCall

### 44. CABLEMAN 1980-1993

O.N. 388618/L.R. 7813884. 4916g, 3369n, 8000d.
116,52 x 17,53 x 7,203 metres.
From *1998:* 4777g, 2446n, 8496d.

16-cyl. 4SA Ruston vee oil engine by Ruston Diesels Ltd., Newton-le-Willows. 4056bhp. 12,5k.

*11.7.1980:* Launched by Appledore Shipbuilders Ltd., Appledore (Yard No. 129) for C. Rowbotham & Sons (Management) Ltd. *10.1980:* Completed. *1981:* Owners became Rowbotham Tankships Ltd. *1987:* Registry transferred to the Isle of Man. *1992:* Owners became Rowbotham Tankships (Gibraltar) Ltd. (Rowbotham Tankships Ltd., managers), Gibraltar. *1.2.1993:* Owners became P&O Tankships (Gibraltar) Ltd. (P&O Tankships Ltd., managers), Gibraltar. *30.12.1996:* P&O Tankships Ltd. acquired by James Fisher & Sons Public Limited Company and vessel transferred to the ownership of James Fisher (Gibraltar) Ltd. (James Fisher Tankships Ltd., managers), retaining Gibraltar registry. *1998:* Renamed LOUGH FISHER. *1999:* Managers became James Fisher (Shipping Services) Ltd. *8.12.2000:* Adrift in Position 52.33.8N, 95.32.5W following an engine breakdown while on passage from Bristol to Milford Haven with refined petroleum products. *10.12.2000:* Arrived in Belfast in tow of tug FIGHTER (BEL, 504g/ 77) for damage assessment after the discharge of cargo. Still in service.


### 45. ECHOMAN 1982-1993

O.N. 703185/L.R. 8111518. 3759g, 2507n, 6125d.
104,30 x 16,72 x 6,812 metres.

12-cyl. 4SA Mirrlees vee oil engine by Mirrlees Blackstone (Stockport) Ltd., Stockport. 3325bhp. 12,5k.

*19.6.1982:* Launched by Appledore Shipbuilders Ltd., Appledore (Yard No. 134) for Rowbotham Tankships Ltd. *9.1982:* Completed. *1987:* Registry transferred to the Isle of Man. *1992:* Owners became Rowbotham Tankships (Hong Kong) Ltd. (Rowbotham Tankships Ltd., managers), Hong Kong. *1.2.1993:* Owners became P&O Tankships (Hong Kong) Ltd. (P&O Tankships Ltd., managers), Hong Kong. *30.12.1996:* P&O Tankships Ltd. acquired by James Fisher & Sons Public Limited Company and vessel transferred to the ownership of James Fisher & Sons Public Limited Company (James Fisher Tankships Ltd., managers), retaining Gibraltar registry. *1997:* Sold to Partrederiet Vivaldi ANS (Th. Jacobsen Management A/S, Sarpsborg, Norway, managers), Norway (NIS) and renamed VIVALDI. Still in service.

ECHOMAN at Eastham                                              Bernard McCall

OILMAN fitting out at Hessle                                        WSS

### 46. OILMAN 1982-1992

O.N. 703198/L.R. 8111568.  997g, 592n, 1563d.  65,51 x 11,36 x 4,079 metres.

6-cyl. 4SA Ruston oil engine by Ruston Diesels Ltd., Newton-le-Willows.
1699bhp.  10,5k.

*6.7.1982:* Launched by R. Dunston (Hessle) Ltd., Hessle (Yard No. 933) for
Rowbotham Tankships Ltd. *11.1982:* Completed. *1987:* Registry transferred
to the Isle of Man. *1992:* Owners became Rowbotham Tankships (Gibraltar)
Ltd. (Rowbotham Tankships Ltd., managers), Gibraltar. *4.12.1992:* Sold to
Pacific Tankship Pty. Ltd., Port Moresby, Papua New Guinea and renamed
PACKULA. *1994:* Managers became Western Tug & Barge Co. Pty. Ltd., Port
Moresby, Papua New Guinea. Still in service.

### 47. HUMBERGATE 1982-1990

O.N. 334104/L.R. 6828765.  1579g, 811n, 2907d.
84,66 x 13,26 x 4,896 metres.

8-cyl. 4SA Ruston oil engine by Ruston & Hornsby Ltd., Lincoln.  2100bhp.

*23.9.1968:* Launched by R. Dunston (Hessle) Ltd., Hessle (Yard No. S858) for
Hull Gates Shipping Co. Ltd. (S.F. Craggs & Co. Ltd., Hull, managers), Hull.
*1.1969:* Completed. *1974:* Managers became Fred Parkes Shipping Co. Ltd.,
Grimsby. *1980:* Managers became Hull Gates Shipping Management Ltd.,
Grimsby. *10.1982:* Share capital in Hull Gates Shipping Co. Ltd. acquired by
Rowbotham Tankships Ltd. and vessel transferred to their ownership. *1987:*
Registry transferred to the Isle of Man. *1990:* Sold to Korinthia Maritime Co.,
Piraeus, Greece and renamed KORINTHIA. *1991:* Managers became Mantinia
Shipping Co., Piraeus, Greece. *1995:* Managers deleted. Still in service.

HUMBERGATE                                    Bernard McCall

## 48. EASTGATE 1982-1993

O.N. 379518/L.R. 7808396.   1599g, 1114n, 3415d.
93,17(BB) x 13,44 x 5,265 metres.

6-cyl. 4SA MaK oil engine by Ube Kosan K.K., Ube.   1655bhp.   12,5k.

*10.3.1979:* Launched by Kanrei Zosen K.K., Naruto (Yard No. 279) for Hull Gates Shipping Co. Ltd. (Fred Parkes Shipping Co. Ltd., Grimsby, managers), Hull. *6.1979:* Completed. *10.1982:* Share capital in Hull Gates Shipping Co. Ltd. acquired by Rowbotham Tankships Ltd. and vessel transferred to their ownership. *1987:* Registry transferred to the Isle of Man. *1992:* Owners became Rowbotham Tankships (Gibraltar) Ltd. (Rowbotham Tankships Ltd., managers), Gibraltar. *1.2.1993:* Owners became P&O Tankships (Gibraltar) Ltd. (P&O Tankships Ltd., managers), Gibraltar. *30.12.1996:* P&O Tankships Ltd. acquired by James Fisher & Sons Public Limited Company and vessel transferred to the ownership of James Fisher (Gibraltar) Ltd. (James Fisher Tankships Ltd., managers), retaining Gibraltar registry. *1999:* Managers became James Fisher (Shipping Services) Ltd. Still in service.

EASTGATE in the Bristol Channel on 26th June 1991        Bernard McCall

### 49. WESTGATE 1982-1993

O.N. 379519/L.R. 7808401. 1599g, 1124n, 3368d.
93,17(BB) x 13,62 x 5,274 metres.
6-cyl. 4SA MaK oil engine by Ube Kosan K.K., Ube. 1655bhp. 12,5k.
*6.6.1979:* Launched by Kanrei Zosen K.K., Naruto (Yard No. 280) for Hull
Gates Shipping Co. Ltd. (Fred Parkes Shipping Co. Ltd., Grimsby, managers),
Hull. *7.1979:* Completed. *1982:* Share capital in Hull Gates Shipping Co. Ltd.
acquired by Rowbotham Tankships Ltd. and vessel transferred to their
ownership. *1987:* Registry transferred to the Isle of Man. *1992:* Owners
became Rowbotham Tankships (Gibraltar) Ltd. (Rowbotham Tankships Ltd.,
managers), Gibraltar. *1.2.1993:* Owners became P&O Tankships (Gibraltar)
Ltd. (P&O Tankships Ltd., managers), Gibraltar. *30.12.1996:* P&O Tankships
Ltd. acquired by James Fisher & Sons Public Limited Company and vessel
transferred to the ownership of James Fisher (Gibraltar) Ltd. (James Fisher
Tankships Ltd., managers), retaining Gibraltar registry. *1999:* Managers
became James Fisher (Shipping Services) Ltd. Still in service.

WESTGATE at Cardiff                                   Bernard McCall

### 50. TANKERMAN 1983-1993

O.N. 703316/L.R. 8116611. 5774g, 4145n, 10716d. 119,72 x 19,23 x 7,751
metres.
From *1998:* 6892g, 3945n. 141,40 x 19,23 x 7,180 metres.

12-cyl. 4SA Mirrlees vee oil engine by Mirrlees Blackstone (Stockport) Ltd.,
Stockport. 4430bhp. 11k.

*28.11.1982:* Launched by Appledore Shipbuilders Ltd., Appledore (Yard No.
135) for Rowbotham Tankships Ltd. *2.1983:* Completed. *1987:* Registry
transferred to the Isle of Man. *1992:* Owners became Rowbotham Tankships
(Gibraltar) Ltd. (Rowbotham Tankships Ltd., managers), Gibraltar. *1.2.1993:*
Owners became P&O Tankships (Gibraltar) Ltd. (P&O Tankships Ltd.,
managers), Gibraltar. *30.12.1996:* P&O Tankships Ltd. acquired by James
Fisher & Sons Public Limited Company and vessel transferred to the
ownership of James Fisher (Gibraltar) Ltd. (James Fisher Tankships Ltd.,
managers), retaining Gibraltar registry. *1998:* Lengthened by Cammell Laird,
Birkenhead, and renamed SEVERN FISHER. *1999:* Managers became James
Fisher (Shipping Services) Ltd. Still in service.

TANKERMAN passing Penarth Head — Bernard McCall

## 51. GUIDESMAN (III) 1989-1993

O.N. 387642/L.R. 7902300. 1421g, 821n, 2162d.
70,82 x 12,73 x 4,711 metres.
From *1995:* 1593g, 938n, 2500d. 79,80 x 12,73 x 4,712 metres.

6-cyl. 4SA Allen oil engine by W.H. Allen, Sons & Co. Ltd., Bedford.
2243bhp. 11,5k.

*14.6.1980:* Launched by Cochrane Shipbuilders Ltd., Selby (Yard No. 111) for Esso Petroleum Co. Ltd., London as ESSO PLYMOUTH. *9.1980:* Completed. *1989:* Acquired by Rowbotham Tankships Ltd., registered in the Isle of Man and renamed GUIDESMAN. *1992:* Owners became Rowbotham Tankships (Gibraltar) Ltd. (Rowbotham Tankships Ltd., managers), Gibraltar. *1.2.1993:* Owners became P&O Tankships (Gibraltar) Ltd. (P&O Tankships Ltd., managers), Gibraltar. *12.1994:* Sold to Hui Quan Pte. Ltd., Singapore and renamed BERJAYA DUA. *1995:* Lengthened by Pan United Shipping Pte. Ltd., Singapore. *1999:* Sold to Prestige Marine Services Plc. Ltd., Singapore. Still in service.

GUIDESMAN (III) at Jersey on 5th February 1989 — Dave Hocquard

## 52. TILLERMAN (III) 1989-1993

O.N. 162652/L.R. 7389168.    7308g, 4861n, 12800d.
142,47 x 17,81 x 7,798 metres.

12-cyl. 2SA Bolnes vee oil engine by N.V. Machinefabriek Bolnes, Krimpen.
5820bhp.  14,5kn.
From *1979:* 8-cyl. 2SA Sulzer oil engine by 'Zgoda' Zaklady Urzadzen
Technicznych, Swietochlowice. 5800bhp.  14,5k.
*19.12.1975:* Launched by Lodose Varv A/B, Lodose (Yard No. 165) for P/R for
m.t. 'Inga' (OT-Rederierna, Skarhamn, managers), Sweden as INGA. *12.1975:*
Completed. *1979:* Managers became Lars Georg Johansson, Skarhamn,
Sweden. *1979:* Re-engined. *1983:* Sold to Bengt Rune I. Bengtsson P/R,
Skarhamn, Sweden and renamed THUNTANK 2. *1986:* Sold to Erik Thun A/B,
Lidkoping, Sweden. *30.12.1987:* Went aground at Krakeskaren, Rivo, during
a voyage from Sundsvall to Grangemouth, and was refloated the same day.
*1989:* Acquired by Rowbotham Tankships Ltd., registered in the Isle of Man
and renamed TILLERMAN. *1992:* Owners became Rowbotham Tankships
(Gibraltar) Ltd. (Rowbotham Tankships Ltd., managers), Gibraltar. *1.2.1993:*
Owners became P&O Tankships (Gibraltar) Ltd. (P&O Tankships Ltd.,
managers), Gibraltar. *30.12.1996:* P&O Tankships Ltd. acquired by James
Fisher & Sons Public Limited Company and vessel transferred to the
ownership of James Fisher (Gibraltar) Ltd. (James Fisher Tankships Ltd.,
managers), retaining Gibraltar registry. *1999:* Sold to Azalea Shipping A/S
(Rederi AB Vaderotank, managers), Norway (NIS) and renamed AZALEA.
Still in service.

TILLERMAN (III)                                                          WSS

### 53. ANCHORMAN (II) 1992-1993

L.R. 9036911. 4842g, 1808n, 6200d. 101,60(BB) x 17,50 x 6,850 metres.

16-cyl. 4SA Blackstone oil engine by Mirrlees Blackstone (Stamford) Ltd., Stamford. 3550bhp. 12,5k.

*17.7.1992:* Launched by Malaysia Shipyard & Engineering Sdn. Bhd., Johore Bahru, Malaysia (Yard No. 054) for Rowbotham Tankships Ltd. *7.1993:* Completed for Antares Navichem Schiffahrtsges., Germany, registered in Liberia and bareboat chartered to P&O Tankships Ltd. *1995:* Sold to Anchorman Shipping Corporation (P&O Tankships Ltd., managers), retaining Liberia registry. *30.12.1996:* P&O Tankships Ltd. acquired by James Fisher & Sons Public Limited Company and James Fisher Tankships Ltd. became managers. *1997:* Sold to Norderhamer Chemikalien Produkten Transport GmbH & Co. m.t. "Antares" KG Nordenham (James Fisher Tankships Ltd., managers), Germany, retaining Liberia registry. *1999:* Managers became James Fisher (Shipping Services) Ltd. Still in service.

ANCHORMAN (II) on the New Waterway                    Dave Hocquard

### 54. CHARTSMAN (III) 1992-1993

L.R. 9036923. 4842g, 1808n, 6397d. 101,60(BB) x 17,52 x 6,850 metres.

16-cyl. 4SA Blackstone oil engine by Mirrlees Blackstone (Stamford) Ltd., Stamford. 3671bhp. 12,5k.

*11.11.1992:* Launched by Malaysia Shipyard & Engineering Sdn. Bhd., Johore Bahru , Malaysia (Yard No. 055) for Rowbotham Tankships Ltd. *10.1993:* Completed for Nordenhamer Chemikalien und Produkten GmbH & Co. m.v. "Chartsman" KG, Germany, registered in Liberia and bareboat chartered to P&O Tankships Ltd. *1995:* Sold to Chartsman Shipping Corporation (P&O Tankships Ltd., managers), retaining Liberia registry. *30.12.1996:* P&O Tankships Ltd. acquired by James Fisher & Sons Public Limited Company and James Fisher Tankships Ltd. became managers. *1999:* Managers became James Fisher (Shipping Services) Ltd. Still in service.

RUDDERMAN (III)                                    Dominic McCall

## 55. RUDDERMAN (III)  1993

L.R. 9050670.   4842g, 1808n, 6397d.   101,60(BB) x 17,52 x 6,850 metres.

16-cyl. 4SA Blackstone oil engine by Mirrlees Blackstone (Stamford) Ltd., Stamford.  3600bhp.  12,5k.

Ordered by Rowbotham Tankships Ltd. *22.4.1993:* Launched by Malaysia Shipyard & Engineering Sdn. Bhd., Johore Bahru, Malaysia (Yard No. 058) for Rudderman Shipping Corporation, registered in Liberia and bareboat chartered to P&O Tankships Ltd. *1.1994:* Completed. *30.12.1996:* P&O Tankships Ltd. acquired by James Fisher & Sons Public Limited Company

RUDDERMAN (III) off Harwich                        Bernard McCall

74

and James Fisher Tankships Ltd. became managers. *1997:* Sold to Nordenhamer Chemikalien und Produkten Transport GmbH & Co. m.t. "Rudderman" KG (James Fisher Tankships Ltd., managers), Germany, retaining Liberia registry. *1999:* Managers became James Fisher (Shipping Services) Ltd. Still in service.

STEERSMAN (V) in New Waterway                    Hocquard/Zwama

## 56. STEERSMAN (V) 1993

L.R. 9050682.   4842g, 1808n, 6397d.   101,60(BB) x 17,52 x 6,850 metres.

16-cyl. 4SA Blackstone oil engine by Mirrlees Blackstone (Stamford) Ltd., Stamford. 3600bhp.   12,5k.

Ordered by Rowbotham Tankships Ltd. *19.8.1993:* Launched by Malaysia Shipyard & Engineering Sdn. Bhd., Johore Bahru, Malaysia (Yard No. 059) for Nordenhamer Chemikalien und Produkten Transport GmbH & Co. m.v. "Steersman" KG, Germany, registered in Liberia and bareboat chartered to P&O Tankships Ltd. *3.1994:* Completed. *1995:* Sold to Steersman Shipping Corporation (P&O Tankships Ltd., managers), retaining Liberia registry. *30.12.1996:* P&O Tankships Ltd. acquired by James Fisher & Sons Public Limited Company and James Fisher Tankships Ltd. became managers. *1997:* Sold to Nordenhamer Chemikalien und Produkten Transport GmbH & Co. m.t. "Steersman" KG (James Fisher Tankships Ltd., managers), Germany, retaining Liberia registry. *1999:* Managers became James Fisher (Shipping Services) Ltd. Still in service.

# P&O TANKSHIPS LTD.

# OWNED SHIPS

| P1. | HELMSMAN (IV) | 1993-1994 |
| | Cf. Owned Ships No. 33. | |

| P2. | BRIDGEMAN (II) | 1993-1994 |
| | Cf. Owned Ships No. 34. | |

| P3. | ASTRAMAN | 1993-1995 |
| | Cf. Owned Ships No. 35. | |

| P4. | POLARISMAN | 1993-1994 |
| | Cf. Owned Ships No. 37. | |

| P5. | ORIONMAN | 1993-1994 |
| | Cf. Owned Ships No. 38. | |

| P6. | OARSMAN (II) | 1993-1996 |
| | Cf. Owned Ships No. 43. | |

| P7. | CABLEMAN | 1993-1996 |
| | Cf. Owned Ships No. 44. | |

| P8. | ECHOMAN | 1993-1996 |
| | Cf. Owned Ships No. 45. | |

| P9. | EASTGATE | 1993-1996 |
| | Cf. Owned Ships No. 48. | |

EASTGATE at Jersey on 15th July 1996                    Dave Hocquard

**P10.  WESTGATE**      1993-1996
Cf. Owned Ships No. 49.

**P11.  TANKERMAN**      1993-1996
Cf. Owned Ships No. 50.

**P12.  GUIDESMAN (III)**      1993-1994
Cf. Owned Ships No. 51.

**P13.  TILLERMAN (III)**      1993-1996
Cf. Owned Ships No. 52.

STELLAMAN (II) at Birkenhead on 29th January 1994          Dave Hocquard

**P14.  STELLAMAN (II)**  1994-1996

L.R. 8007121.   1599g, 1168n, 3679d.   97,80(BB) x 13,75 x 5,779 metres.
6-cyl. 4SA MaK oil engine by MaK Maschinenbau GmbH, Kiel.
2250bhp.   12,75k.

*13.9.1980:* Launched by Schiffswerft und Maschinenfabrik Paul Lindenau GmbH & Co. KG, Kiel (Yard No. 190) for Partenreederei m.s. 'Richard' (DS-Tankschiff Reederei GmbH & Co. KG, Bremen, managers), Federal Republic of Germany as RICHARD. *11.1980:* Completed. *1988:* Sold to Partenreederei m.t. 'Navajo' (Atlantic-Rhederei F. & W. Joch KG, Hamburg, managers), Federal Republic of Germany and renamed NAVAJO. *1989:* Flag transferred to Antigua & Barbuda. *1993:* Registry transferred to Liberia. *14.1.1994:* Acquired by P&O Tankships (Hong Kong) Ltd. (P&O Tankships Ltd., managers), Hong Kong and renamed STELLAMAN. *30.12.1996:* P&O Tankships Ltd. acquired by James Fisher & Sons Public Limited Company and vessel transferred to the ownership of James Fisher (Gibraltar) Ltd. (James Fisher Tankships Ltd., managers), retaining Gibraltar registry. *1999:* Managers became James Fisher (Shipping Services) Ltd. Still in service.

IRISHGATE in Hull Gates' colours                    Dave Hocquard

## P15. IRISHGATE 1994-1996

O.N. 379537/L.R. 8009430.  1599g, 1124n, 3290d.
93,15(BB) x 13,44 x 5,193 metres.
6-cyl. 4SA MaK oil engine by Ube Kosan K.K., Ube.  2250bhp.  12,5k.
*24.1.1981:* Launched by Kanrei Zosen K.K., Naruto (Yard No. 291) for
Portland Overseas Shipping Ltd., London and bareboat chartered to Hull
Gates Shipping Co. Ltd., Hull. *5.1981:* Completed. *1.1982:* Sold to Turnbull
Scott Shipping Co. Ltd., Farnborough and bareboat charter transferred to
Rowbotham Tankships Ltd. *1987:* Registry transferred to the Isle of Man.
*1991:* Sold to Aber River Shipping Ltd. (Rowbotham Tankships Ltd.,
managers), retaining Isle of Man registry. *1992:* Registry transferred to
Gibraltar. *18.1.1993:* Managers became P&O Tankships Ltd. *31.5.1994:*
Acquired by P&O Tankships (Gibraltar) Ltd. (P&O Tankships Ltd., managers),
Gibraltar. *30.12.1996:* P&O Tankships Ltd. acquired by James Fisher & Sons
Public Limited Company and vessel transferred to the ownership of James
Fisher (Gibraltar) Ltd. (James Fisher Tankships Ltd., managers), retaining
Gibraltar registry. *1999:* Managers became James Fisher (Shipping Services)
Ltd. Still in service.

IRISHGATE outward bound from Jersey on 30th Nov. 1996    Dave Hocquard

## P16. NORTHGATE 1994-1996

O.N. 379536/L.R. 8004612. 1599g, 1124n, 3290d.
93,15(BB) x 13,42 x 5,200 metres.
6-cyl. 4SA MaK oil engine by Ube Kosan K.K., Ube. 2250bhp. 12,5k.

*4.10.1980:* Launched by Kanrei Zosen K.K., Naruto (Yard No. 289) for Finance For Industry Ltd., London and bareboat chartered to Hull Gates Shipping Co. Ltd., Hull. *1.1981:* Completed. *1982:* Owners became Investors in Industry Plc. (3is), London. *11.1982:* Bareboat charter transferred to Rowbotham Tankships Ltd. *1987:* Registry transferred to the Isle of Man. *1991:* Sold to Luzon Sea Shipping Ltd. (Rowbotham Tankships Ltd., managers), retaining Isle of Man registry. *1992:* Registry transferred to Gibraltar. *18.1.1993:* Managers became P&O Tankships Ltd. *31.5.1994:* Acquired by P&O Tankships (Gibraltar) Ltd. (P&O Tankships Ltd., managers), Gibraltar. *30.12.1996:* P&O Tankships Ltd. acquired by James Fisher & Sons Public Limited Company and vessel transferred to the ownership of James Fisher (Gibraltar) Ltd. (James Fisher Tankships Ltd., managers), retaining Gibraltar registry. *1999:* Managers became James Fisher (Shipping Services) Ltd. Still in service.

NORTHGATE at Jersey on 20th November 1993          Dave Hocquard


## P17. QUARTERMAN (III) 1996

O.N. 730217/L.R. 9118159. 3368g, 1039n, 3700d.
91,00(BB) x 15,60 x 5,100 metres.
6-cyl. 4SA MaK oil engine by Krupp MaK Maschinenbau GmbH, Kiel. 3589bhp. 12,1k.

*23.1.1996:* Launched by Qiuxin Shipyard, Shanghai (Yard No. 1243) for P&O Tankships Ltd. as QUARTERMAN. *12.1996:* Completed. *30.12.1996:* P&O Tankships Ltd. acquired by James Fisher & Sons Public Limited Company and vessel transferred to the ownership of James Fisher Tankships Ltd. *1997:* Renamed FORTH FISHER. *1999:* Managers became James Fisher (Shipping Services) Ltd. Still in service.

### P18. WHEELSMAN (IV) 1996

O.N. 900119/L.R. 9118161.    3368g, 1039n, 3700d.
91,00(BB) x 15,60 x 5,000 metres.
6-cyl. 4SA MaK oil engine by Krupp MaK Maschinenbau GmbH, Kiel.
3589bhp.    12,1k.
*2.4.1996:* Launched by Qiuxin Shipyard, Shanghai (Yard No. 1244) for P&O
Tankships Ltd. as WHEELSMAN. *30.12.1996:* P&O Tankships Ltd. acquired by
James Fisher & Sons Public Limited Company. *6.1997:* Completed for James
Fisher Tankships Ltd. as GALWAY FISHER. *1999:* Managers became James
Fisher (Shipping Services) Ltd. Still in service.

SOLENT FISHER, ex Bridgeman (III) inward bound to Jersey    Dave Hocquard

### P19. BRIDGEMAN (III) 1996

O.N. 900562/L.R. 9118173.    3368g, 1039n, 3700d.
91,00(BB) x 15,63 x 5,000 metres.
6-cyl. 4SA MaK oil engine by Krupp Mak Maschinenbau GmbH, Kiel.
3589bhp.    12,1k.
*12.12.1996:* Launched by Qiuxin Shipyard, Shanghai (Yard No. 1245) for P&O
Tankships Ltd. as BRIDGEMAN. *30.12.1996:* P&O Tankships Ltd. acquired by
James Fisher & Sons Public Limited Company. *10.1997:* Completed for
James Fisher Tankships Ltd. as SOLENT FISHER. *1999:* Managers became
James Fisher (Shipping Services) Ltd. Still in service.

### P20. HELMSMAN (V) 1996

O.N.900709/L.R. 9118185.    3368g, 1039n, 3700d.
91,00(BB) x 15,60 x 5,000 metres.
6-cyl. 4SA MaK oil engine by MaK Motoren GmbH & Co. KG,  Kiel.
3589bhp.    21,1k.
Ordered by P&O Tankships Ltd. to be named HELMSMAN. *30.12.1996:* P&O
Tankships Ltd. acquired by James Fisher & Sons Public Limited Company.
*10.3.1997:* Launched by Qiuxin Shipyard, Shanghai (Yard No. 1246) for
James Fisher & Sons Public Limited Company as  MILFORD FISHER. *3.1998:*
Completed. *1999:* Managers became James Fisher (Shipping Services) Ltd.
Still in service.

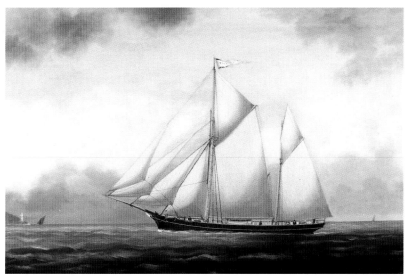

PRINCESS painting by A.K. Branden          Andrew Huckett Collection

ELSIE painting by A.K. Branden          Andrew Huckett Collection

RUDDERMAN (I)                                                                    WSS

ANCHORMAN (I) off the Lizard in 1968                              Ambrose Greenway

BRIDGEMAN (I)                                      Chriss Reynolds Collection

BRIDGEMAN (II) at the Isle of Grain in 1988                Chriss Reynolds

LOUGH FISHER, ex Cableman                     Bernard McCall

IRISHGATE at Shoreham in November 1992        Chriss Reynolds

NORTHGATE at Jersey on 4th September 1989          Dave Hocquard

CHARTSMAN (III) off Portishead on 5th August 1996          Bernard McCall

RUDDERMAN (III) off Portishead                    Bernard McCall

STEERSMAN (V) on the New Waterway            Hocquard/Zwama

FORTH FISHER, ex Quarterman (III) on the river Tees          Bernard McCall
on 14th August 1997

GALWAY FISHER, ex Wheelsman (IV) at Milford Haven          Des Davies
on 17th February 2000

SOLENT FISHER, ex Bridgeman (III) in Milford Docks      Des Davies
on 31st May 1998

MILFORD FISHER, ex Helmsman (V) at Milford Haven     Des Davies

# VESSELS MANAGED ON BEHALF OF THE BRITISH AND UNITED STATES GOVERNMENTS

## M1. MOTOR LIGHTERS 1916-1919

Designed by James Pollock, Sons & Co. Ltd.
Owners: The Admiralty.
Managed by C. Rowbotham & Sons at various times between *17.2.1916* and *19.7.1919*.

### X57.

O.N. 166786/L.R. 5113539.  105' 6" x 21' 0" x 7' 6".
From *1938:* 152g, 54n, 200d.  110' 0" x 21' 4" x 8' 0".
From *1964:* 186g, 64n, 279d.  33,53 x 6,51 x 2,439 metres.
60bhp Skandia oil engine.
From *1938:* 2-cyl. 2SA oil engine by Skandiaverken A/B, Lysekil.
*1915:* Completed by Sunderland Shipbuilding Co. Ltd., South Dock, Sunderland for the Admiralty (C. Rowbotham & Sons, managers). Converted into a dumb barge. *1938:* Owners given as J.J. Prior (Transport) Ltd., London, converted into a general cargo coaster, re-engined and renamed FENCE. *1964:* Rebuilt and renamed PETER P. *1998:* Renamed J.J. PRIOR and laid up on river Medway pending possible preservation. Purchased for conversion into a floating home in London's Docklands.

### X36, X37, X38, X63, X64, X69, X74, X76, X81, X86, X95, X133, X149, X151, X178, X198, X201, X203. X204, X205, X207, X208, X209, X210, X211, X213, X216, X217, 218, X221, X222, X223, X224 and X225.

Built at various yards but few or no details are known.

## M2. LORD DEVONPORT 1916-1921 Hopper barge

O.N. 135239.  970g, 385n, 1482d.  200.4 x 34.1 x 16.9 feet.
T.3-cyl. steam engine by Lobnitz & Co. Ltd., Renfrew.
*7.1913:* Completed by Lobnitz & Co. Ltd., Renfrew (Yard No. 757) for The General Works Construction Co. Ltd., London. *1916:* Owners given as S. Pearson & Sons Ltd. (C. Rowbotham & Sons, managers), London. *3.4.1916-26.3.1918:* In use as Expeditionary Force Transport. *27.3.1918-23.4.1918:* In use as a collier. *24.4.1918-1921:* In use as Expeditionary Force Transport. *1921:* Sold to Union Government of South Africa (South African Railways & Harbours Administration), South Africa and renamed MOLLY MAWK. *1961:* Owners became the Republic of South Africa. *1966:* Sold to K. Nathan (Pty.) Ltd., South Africa and broken up at Durban.

LORD DEVONPORT National Maritime Museum

**M3. LORD RITCHIE** 1916-1921 Hopper barge

O.N. 135245. 971g, 386n, 1482d. 200.4 x 34.1 x 16.9 feet.

T.3-cyl. steam engine by Lobnitz & Co. Ltd., Renfrew.

*7.1913:* Completed by Lobnitz & Co. Ltd., Renfrew (Yard No. 758) for The General Works Construction Co. Ltd., London. *1916:* Owners given as S. Pearson & Sons Ltd. (C. Rowbotham & Sons, managers), London. *3.4.1916-26.3.1918:* In use as Expeditionary Force Transport. *27.3.1918-15.4.1918:* In use as a collier. *30.4.1918-1921:* In use as Expeditionary Force Transport. *1921:* Sold to Union Government of South Africa (South African Railway & Harbours Administration), South Africa and renamed DUYKER. *1961:* Owners became the Republic of South Africa. *1965:* Broken up at East London.

**M4. LORD PURFLEET** 1917-1920 Floating derrick

583g.

Owners: Port of London Authority (C. Rowbotham & Sons, managers). *19.2.1917-13.12.1920:* In use as Expeditionary Force Transport on the River Thames.

**M5. RECTOR** 1917-1919 Tug

O.N. 140264. 106g, 1n. 73.3 x 20.0 x 10.2 feet.

T.3-cyl. steam engine by Plenty & Sons Ltd., Newbury.

*1916:* Completed by Rennie Forrestt Shipbuilding, Engineering & Dry Dock Co. Ltd., Wivenhoe (Yard No. 1251) for Cory Colliers Ltd., London. *2.6.1917-22.10.1919:* In use as military tug based in Dunkirk with C. Rowbotham & Sons as agents. *1921:* Returned to owners. *1922:* Owners became Cory Lighterage Ltd., London. *1923:* Owners became R. & J.H. Rea., Southampton. *1937:* Owners became Rea Ltd. *1939:* Owners became R. & J.H. Rea Ltd. *22.6.1942:* Damaged by German aircraft at Southampton. *1946:* Owners became Cory Lighterage Ltd., London. *1952:* Owners became R. & J.H. Rea Ltd. *1954:* Owners became Wm. Cory & Son Ltd., London. *1954:* Sold for breaking up.

## M6. LORD NORTHFLEET 1918-1920 Hopper barge 486g.

Owners: Messrs. Constants Ltd. (C. Rowbotham & Sons, managers). *26.7.1918-3.7.1920:* In use as Expeditionary Force Transport on Rochester service.

SAINT TUDNO National Maritime Museum

## M7. SAINT TUDNO 1918-1919 Paddle steamer

O.N. 97861. 754g, 339n. 265.4 x 32.6 x 11.4 feet.

2-cyl. CD steam engine by Fairfield Shipbuilding and Engineering Co. Ltd., Glasgow.

*1891:* Completed by Fairfield Shipbuilding and Engineering Co. Ltd., Glasgow (Yard No. 360) for Liverpool & North Wales Steamship Co. Ltd., Liverpool. *1911:* Sold to MacIver Steamship Co. Ltd. (T.W. Tamplin, managers), Liverpool. In use as a tender at Southampton for Hamburg-Amerika Line. *7.1914:* Commandeered and placed under management of Southampton, Isle of Wight & South of England Royal Mail Steam Packet Co. *24.9.1914-9.10.1918:* In use as Expeditionary Force Transport between Southampton and France. *5.1918:* Managers became C. Rowbotham & Sons. *10.10.1918-18.9.1919:* In use on American Government Naval Service. *18.9.1919:* Returned to Admiralty Marshal. *1922:* Sold to T.C. Pas for breaking up at Scheveningen.

### M8. LORD POPLAR 1919-1920 Hopper barge

869g.

Owners: Clyde Harbour Commissioners. - -*9.8.1919:* In use as Expeditionary Force Transport. *10.8.1919-17.8.1919:* In use as a collier. *18.8.1919-14.9.1920:* In use as Expeditionary Force Transport on coasting service. C. Rowbotham & Sons acted as agents.

### M9. LORD TILBURY 1919-1920 Hopper barge

874g.

Owners: Clyde Harbour Commissioners. - -*24.11.1919:* In use as Expeditionary Force Transport between London and France. *25.11.1919- - :* In use as Expeditionary Force Transport in UK ports. *31.1.1920:* Sold to The Shipping Controller. C. Rowbotham & Sons acted as agents.

### M10. ST. TEATH 1919-1921 Saint class rescue tug

O.N. 144321. 417g, 2nt. 135.0 x 29.0 x 13.7 feet.

T.3-cyl. steam engine by G.K. Stothert & Co. Ltd., Bristol.

*29.5.1919:* Launched by C.H. Walker and Co. Ltd., Sudbrook (Yard No. 239) for The Shipping Controller (C. Rowbotham & Sons, managers), London. *11.1919:* Completed. *1920:* Laid up. *1926:* Sold to Brazilian Government and renamed PARANA. *1930/31:* Deleted from Lloyd's Register.

### M11. ST. TUDY 1919-1921 Saint class rescue tug

O.N. 144439. 417g, 2nt. 135.0 x 29.0 x 13.7 feet.

T.3-cyl. steam engine by G.K. Stothert & Co. Ltd., Bristol.

*11.11.1919:* Launched by C.H. Walker and Co. Ltd., Sudbrook (Yard No. 240) for The Shipping Controller (C. Rowbotham & Sons, managers), London. *1.1920:* Completed. *1920:* Laid up. *1926:* Sold to F.P. Barney & Co. Ltd., London and renamed ST. EILEEN. *1926:* Sold to Brazilian Government. *1930/31:* Deleted from Lloyd's Register.

### M12. NEPTUNIA 1938-1939 Tug

O.N. 160534. 798g, 53n. 173.9 x 35.7 feet.

T.3-cyl. steam engine by C.D. Holmes & Co. Ltd., Hull.

*2.5.1938:* Launched by Cochrane & Sons Ltd., Selby (Yard No. 1194) for Overseas Towage & Salvage Co. Ltd. (C. Rowbotham & Sons, managers), London. *8.1938:* Completed. *9.9.1939:* Hired for service by the Admiralty. *13.9.1939:* Sunk by torpedo and gunfire from the German submarine U 29 in position 49° 20'N 14° 40'W after leaving Falmouth to carry out salvage work in the North Atlantic.

## M13. SALVONIA 1939-1940 Tug

O.N. 167155.  571g, 33n.  143.6 x 33.1 x 15.2 feet.

T.3-cyl. steam engine by C.D. Holmes & Co. Ltd., Hull.

*26.9.1938:* Launched by Cochrane & Sons Ltd., Selby (Yard No. 1197) for Overseas Towage & Salvage Co. Ltd. (C. Rowbotham & Sons, managers), London. *1.1939:* Completed. *9.1939-14.10.1945:* Hired for service as a rescue tug by the Admiralty [Pennant No. W43]. *1940:* Rowbotham management ceased. *10.1945:* Returned to owners by the Admiralty. *1947:* Transferred to Compagnie de Remorquage et de Sauvetage "Les Abeilles", France and renamed ABEILLE No. 25. *1967:* Transferred to Compagnie Cherbourgeoise de Remorquage et de Sauvetage, France. *1968:* Sold to Société Progemar, France. *2.1970:* Sold to Etablissements Fablon, France for breaking up. *4.1970:* Demolition commenced at Le Havre.


## M14. NEREIDIA 1939 Tug

O.N. 167180.  327g.  119.7 x 29.2 x 13.2 feet.

T.3-cyl. steam engine by C.D. Holmes & Sons Ltd., Hull.

*26.10.1938:* Launched by Cochrane & Sons Ltd., Selby (Yard No. 1198) for Overseas Towage & Salvage Co. Ltd. (C. Rowbotham & Sons, managers), London. *2.1939:* Completed. *3.1939:* Sold to Compagnie de Remorquage et de Sauvetage "Les Abeilles", France and renamed ABEILLE No. 4. *3.7.1940:* Seized and taken over by the Ministry of Shipping (Overseas Towage & Salvage Co. Ltd., managers), London. *8.1940-20.12.1945:* In use on miscellaneous naval duties as a rescue tug [Pennant No. W94]. *1941:* Owners became the Ministry of War Transport. *1946:* Returned to French owners. *1967:* Sold to Rimorchiatori Sardi S.p.A., Italy and renamed SPARVIERO. *1986:* Sold to shipbreakers in Italy.

SABINE                                    Andrew Huckett Collection

## M15. SABINE 1940 Tug

O.N. 180600. 488g, 252n. 148.0 x 26.0 x 16.0 feet.

T.3-cyl. steam engine.

*1917:* Completed by Spedden Shipbuilding Co., Baltimore (Yard No. 248) for Freeport Sulphur Transportation Co., United States of America as FREEPORT SULPHUR No. 2. *1930:* Sold to Sabine Transportation Co. Inc. (M.T. Ball, manager), United States of America and renamed SABINE. *1931:* Owners became Sabine Transportation Co. Inc. (M.T. Ball, manager), United States of America. *1940:* Acquired by Overseas Towage & Salvage Co. Ltd. (C. Rowbotham & Sons, managers), London. *1940:* Sold to the Admiralty as a rescue tug [Pennant No. W74]. *1944:* Transferred to the Ministry of War Transport. *1945:* Sold to Salvedor Co. Ltd. (Philip Bauer, manager), London. *1949:* Manager became Alexander Charles Grant. *1950:* Sold to H.G. Pounds, Portsmouth. *1950:* Sold to British Iron and Steel Corporation and allocated to J.J. King & Co. for breaking up. *6.11.1950:* Demolition commenced at Gateshead.

## M16. SEA GIANT 1940 Tug

508g, 277n. 148.3 x 30.0 x 15.1 feet.

T.3-cyl. steam engine.

*12.1.1920:* Launched by Staten Island Shipbuilding Co., Mariners Harbour, New York (Yard No. 706) for the United States Navy as CONTOCOOK. *20.8.1920:* Commissioned. *27.11.1933:* Decommissioned. *1934:* Sold to unspecified owners, United States of America. *1937:* Sold to Shipowners & Merchants Tugboat Co., United States of America and renamed SEA GIANT. *1940:* Acquired by Overseas Towage & Salvage Co. Ltd. (C. Rowbotham & Sons, managers), London. *4.6.1940:* Left Los Angeles for the United Kingdom. *1940:* Sold to the Admiralty as a rescue tug [Pennant No. W125]. *7.1946:* Transferred to the Ministry of War Transport and laid up. *1948:* Sold to Garnet W. Stevens, United States of America. *1949/50:* Deleted from Lloyd's Register.

## M17. EMPIRE FIRTH 1941-1942 General cargo

O.N. 166688. 315g, 145n. 131.5 x 24.6 x 8.8 feet.

6-cyl. 2SA Crossley oil engine by Crossley Brothers Ltd., Manchester.

*3.1941:* Launched by Richards Ironworks Ltd., Lowestoft (Yard No. 280) for the Ministry of War Transport (C. Rowbotham & Sons, managers), London. *29.8.1941:* Completed. *29.8.1941-19.11.1941:* In use in coasting and short sea trade. *20.11.1941-15.5.1944:* In use as an armament store carrier. *1942:* Managers became John Campbell, Irvine. *16.5.1944-13.11.1945:* In use in coastal and short sea trade. *11.1945:* Sold to John Campbell, Irvine. *1947:* Renamed ANNICK. *1954:* Sold to A/S Lo-Nes Rederi (Thore Horve & Johns Sandvik, managers), Norway and renamed LONES. *1958:* Sold to Rose Line Ltd. (Thomas Rose & Co., managers), Sunderland and renamed EDENSIDE. *1967:* Sold to North East by East Shipping Co. Ltd., London and renamed NORTH TRADER. *1968:* Sold to N. Jadavji & S.G. Hirji, Kenya. *1969:* Sold to United Youth Shipping Co., Tanzania and renamed TANZANIA. Abandoned on beach front, Dar es Salaam. *1.1995:* Demolition commenced after being sold to Tanzania breakers.

## M18. EMPIRE MAPLE 1941-1947 Maple class tug

O.N. 168772. 129g. 92.5 x 20.5 x 8.4 feet.

T.3-cyl. steam engine by McKie & Baxter Ltd., Paisley.

*20.5.1941:* Launched by R. Dunston Ltd., Thorne (Yard No. T358) for the Ministry of War Transport (C. Rowbotham & Sons, managers), London. *2.9.1941:* Completed. *2.9.1941-15.12.1943/16.12.1943-10.11.1944/3.12.1944-1945:* In use on naval duties. *1.4.1946:* Owners became the Ministry of Transport. *1947:* Sold to the Government of Poland (Gdynia-America Shipping Lines Ltd., managers), Poland and renamed TARPAN. *1948:* Managers became Zegluga Polska S.A. *1951:* Management ceased. *1959:* Managers became Zarzad Portu Gdanska. *c.1961:* Believed broken up.

## M19. EMPIRE GARNET/EMPIRE LAD 1941-1946

O.N. 168217. 298g, 105n. 127.7 x 24.2 x 10.2 feet.

5-cyl. 2SA oil engine by British Auxiliaries Ltd., Glasgow.

*10.7.1941:* Launched by Rowhedge Ironworks Co. Ltd., Rowhedge (Yard No. 601) for the Ministry of War Transport (C. Rowbotham & Sons, managers), London as EMPIRE GARNET. *10.1941:* Completed as EMPIRE LAD. *31.10.1941-17.7.1946:* In use as a tanker on coastal and short sea duties. *1.4.1946:* Owners became the Ministry of Transport. *18.7.1946:* Sold to Anglo-American Oil Co. Ltd., London and renamed ESSO SUWANEE. *1947:* Owners became Esso Transportation Co. Ltd., London. *1951:* Owners became Esso Petroleum Co. Ltd. *1960:* Sold to P.L. Den Breejen, Netherlands. *1963:* Sold to Compañia. de Comercio y Naviera Alpes S.A., Panama, converted to general cargo and renamed U.S.A. *1966:* Sold to Antco S.A., Panama and renamed PEJEREY. *1966:* Renamed ESTEREL. *1969:* Sold to Colombo Shipping Corporation, Panama and renamed WESTEREND. *1970:* Sold to Albina S.A., Panama and renamed SUNRISE. *1970:* Renamed GRACE. *1971:* Sold to Dionisios P. Gousetis, John Stylianos Bastas, Marios D. Avouris & Panaghiotis D. Lappos, Greece and renamed CAPTAIN STELIOS. *1975:* Sold to Constantinos Dagadakis, Greece and renamed SAN LIBERAL. *1977:* Sold to E. & G. Kottis & S. Valsamidis, Greece and renamed KLEOPATRA. Continued existence in doubt.

EMPIRE LAD                                                                    WSS

### M20. EMPIRE LASS 1941-1944

O.N. 168794.   813g, 333n.   193.0 x 30.7 x 13.8 feet.
From *1957:* 877g, 416n.   230.5 x 30.75 x 12.8 feet.

T.3-cyl. steam engine by Aitchison, Blair Ltd., Clydebank.

*31.7.1941:* Launched by Grangemouth Dockyard Co. Ltd., Grangemouth (Yard No. 435) for the Ministry of War Transport (C. Rowbotham & Sons, managers), London. *8.12.1941:* Completed. *8.12.1941-22.2.1944:* In use as a tanker in coastal and short sea trade. *1944:* Managers became Anglo-Saxon Petroleum Co. Ltd., London. *23.2.1944-14.8.1946:* In use as a water carrier. *1.4.1946:* Owners became the Ministry of Transport. *1946:* Sold to Anglo-American Oil Co. Ltd., London and renamed ESSO JUNIATA. *1951:* Owners became Esso Petroleum Co. Ltd. *1956:* Sold to F.T. Everard & Sons Ltd., London and renamed ARGOSITY. *1957:* Lengthened. *1969:* Sold to Brugse Scheepsloperij, Belgium. *6.5.1969:* Arrived at Bruges for breaking up.

EMPIRE TEAK                                                    J.W. Kennedy

### M21. EMPIRE TEAK 1942-1950 Birch class tug

O.N. 167119.   242g.   106.7 x 26.7 x 11.6 feet.

T.3-cyl. steam engine by C.D. Holmes & Co. Ltd., Hull.

*21.12.1941:* Launched by Henry Scarr Ltd., Hessle (Yard No. S420) for the Ministry of War Transport (C. Rowbotham & Sons, managers), London. *14.4.1942:* Completed. *14.4.1942-22.8.1950:* In use on naval duties. *1.4.1946:* Owners became the Ministry of Transport. *23.8.1950:* Sold to Alexandra Towing Co. Ltd., Liverpool and renamed BRAMBLES. *1969:* Sold to Northern Slipways Ltd., Irish Republic. *24.8.1971:* Arrived at Briton Ferry to be broken up by T.W. Ward Ltd.

## M22. EMPIRE RACE 1942-45/1951-1962 Birch class tug

O.N. 167121. 242g. 106.7 x 26.7 x 11.6 feet.

T.3-cyl. steam engine by C.D. Holmes & Co. Ltd., Hull.

*21.11.1941:* Launched by Henry Scarr Ltd., Hessle (Yard No. S421) for the Ministry of War Transport (C. Rowbotham & Sons, managers), London. *1.6.1942:* Completed. *1.6.1942-13.2.1944:* In use on naval duties. *14.2.1944-10.1944:* In use on coastal towing duties. *10.1944-30.11.1945:* In use on naval duties. *1.12.1945:* Taken over by the Admiralty for naval duties at Harwich. *1.4.1946:* Owners became the Ministry of Transport. *1951:* Managers became C. Rowbotham & Sons. *1956:* Managers became C. Rowbotham & Sons (Management) Ltd. *1958:* Released from service. *1958:* Owners became the Ministry of Transport & Civil Aviation. *1962:* Sold to Capieci Societa di Navigazione S.p.A., Italy and renamed CAPO D'ORLANDO. *1969:* Owners became Capieci S.p.A. Societa di Navigazione e Rimorchiatori e Salvataggi. *1986:* Sold to the Italian Navy. Believed to be still in service.

## M23. EMPIRE ARTHUR 1942

O.N. 168798. 784g, 349n. 193.0 x 30.7 x 14.1 feet.

T.3-cyl. steam engine by D. Rowan & Co. Ltd., Glasgow.

*5.3.1942:* Launched by Grangemouth Dockyard Co. Ltd., Grangemouth (Yard No. 439) for the Ministry of War Transport (C. Rowbotham & Sons, managers), London. *30.5.1942:* Completed. *30.5.1942-6.10.1942:* In use as a tanker in coastal and short sea trade. *1942:* Managers became Bulk Oil Steamship Co. Ltd., London. *7.10.1942-22.11.1943:* In use as a water carrier. *22.11.1943:* Capsized and sunk alongside Kissy Jetty, Freetown, while loading water. Removed, beached, refloated and repaired. *1.4.1946:* Owners became the Ministry of Transport. *1949:* Sold to "Ape" Azionaria Petroliere, Italy and renamed MERULA. *1951:* Sold to F.T. Everard & Sons Ltd., London and renamed ADHERITY. *1962:* Sold to N.V. Machine & Scheepsloperij 'De Koophandel' for breaking up at Nieuwe Lekkerland, Netherlands.

## M24. EMPIRE DAMSEL 1942-1945

O.N. 168800. 784g, 349n. 193.0 x 30.7 x 14.1 feet.

T.3-cyl. steam engine by D. Rowan & Co. Ltd., Glasgow.

*29.6.1942:* Launched by Grangemouth Dockyard Co. Ltd., Grangemouth (Yard No. 441) for the Ministry of War Transport (C. Rowbotham & Sons, managers), London. *21.9.1942:* Completed. *21.9.1942-8.10.1942:* In use as a tanker. *9.10.1942-30.11.1942:* In use as a water carrier. *1.12.1942-18.5.1943:* In use as a tanker in coastal and short sea trade. *19.5.1943-28.2.1947:* In use as a tanker. *1945:* Managers became Anglo-Saxon Petroleum Co. Ltd., London. *1.4.1946:* Owners became the Ministry of Transport and managers became Bulk Oil Steamship Co. Ltd., London. *1947:* Sold to Bulk Oil Steamship Co. Ltd., London and renamed PASS OF BALMAHA. *1965:* Sold to Cory Maritime Ltd., London. *1966:* Chartered for use as a storage hulk at Dundalk. *19.2.1967:* Arrived at Glasgow in tow for breaking up by W.H. Arnott Young & Co. Ltd.

### M25. EMPIRE TOBY 1942-1947 Maple class tug

O.N. 168787. 129g. 92.5 x 20.5 x 8.4 feet.

T.3-cyl. steam engine by Worsley Mesnes Ironworks Ltd., Wigan.

*8.7.1942:* Launched by R. Dunston Ltd., Thorne (Yard No. T376) for the Ministry of War Transport (C. Rowbotham & Sons, managers), London. *27.8.1942:* Completed. *27.8.1942-26.11.1944:* In use on naval duties. *28.11.1944-1947:* In use on naval duties. *1.4.1946:* Owners became the Ministry of Transport. *1947:* Sold to Union des Remorquers de l'Ocean, France and renamed CROISIC. *1965:* Sold to Société Mir Deros, France. *1965:* Sold to Société "Les Goelands", France. *1969:* Sold to Algero-Provencale de Remorquage, France. *1971:* Owners became Société Algero-Provencale de Remorquage and renamed CROISIC I. *1973:* Sold to Cantieri Navali Santa Maria, Italy. *27.2.1973:* Towed to La Spezia for breaking up. *12.1973:* Demolition commenced.

### M26. EMPIRE GYPSY 1942-1945

O.N. 168737. 813g, 333n. 193.0 x 30.7 x 13.8 feet.

T.3-cyl. steam engine by D. Rowan & Co. Ltd., Glasgow.

*31.8.1942:* Launched by A. & J. Inglis Ltd., Glasgow (Yard No. 1175P) for the Ministry of War Transport (C. Rowbotham & Sons, managers), London. *11.11.1942:* Completed. *11.11.1942-30.11.1942:* In use as a water carrier. *1.12.1942-1.3.1948:* In use as a tanker in coastal and short sea trade. *1945:* Managers became Anglo-Saxon Petroleum Co. Ltd., London. *1.4.1946:* Owners became the Ministry of Transport. *1947:* Managers became Bulk Oil Steamship Co. Ltd., London. *1948:* Sold to the Indian Navy and renamed SAMBHAR. *1968:* In service as a dockyard craft. *1976:* Deleted from Navy List.

### M27. EMPIRE FRANK 1942-1944 Warrior class tug

O.N. 169032. 260g. 107.8 x 12.5 feet.

T.3-cyl. steam engine by Swan, Hunter & Wigham Richardson Ltd., Newcastle upon Tyne.

*2.9.1942:* Launched by J. Crown & Sons Ltd., Sunderland (Yard No. 206) for the Ministry of War Transport (C. Rowbotham & Sons, managers), London. *6.11.1942:* Completed. *6.11.1942-12.5.1946:* In use on naval duties. *1944:* Managers became Steel & Bennie Ltd., Glasgow. *1.4.1946:* Owners became the Ministry of Transport. *13.5.1946:* Sold to Steel & Bennie Ltd., Glasgow and renamed BRIGADIER. *21.2.1960:* Grounded on Horse Island, off Ardrossan. *21.4.1960:* Declared a constructive total loss.

### M28. EMPIRE SERAPH 1942-1947 Maple class tug

O.N. 169077. 129g. 92.5 x 20.5 x 8.4 feet.

T.3-cyl. steam engine by Crabtree (1931) Ltd., Great Yarmouth.

*25.10.1942:* Launched by R. Dunston Ltd., Thorne (Yard No. T374) for the Ministry of War Transport (C. Rowbotham & Sons, managers), London. *22.12.1942:* Completed. *22.12.1942-21.5.1944:* In use on naval duties. *22.5.1944-9.8.1944:* In use on coastal towing duties. *10.8.1944-1947:* In use on naval duties. *1.4.1946:* Owners became the Ministry of Transport. *1947:* Sold to Gdynia-America Shipping Lines Ltd., Poland and renamed BIZON. *1951:* Taken over by the Polish Government. *1959:* Managers became Zarzad Portu Szczecin. *c.1960:* Believed broken up.

## M29. EMPIRE HOMESTEAD 1943-1946

O.N. 168389. 296g, 103n. 127.7 x 24.2 x 10.2 feet.
From 1963: 370g, 148n, 438d. 156' 6" x 24' 1" x 9' 10 ".

5-cyl. 2SA oil engine by British Auxiliaries Ltd., Glasgow.

*10.11.1942:* Launched by Rowhedge Ironworks Co. Ltd., Rowhedge (Yard No. 607) for the Ministry of War Transport (C. Rowbotham & Sons, managers), London. *12.2.1943:* Completed. *12.2.1943-16.5.1944:* In use as a tanker on coastal and short sea duties. *17.5.1944-25.4.1945:* In use as a water carrier. *26.4.1945-11.7.1946:* In use as a tanker. *1.4.1946:* Owners became the Ministry of Transport. *12.7.1946:* Sold to A/S Norske Shell, Norway and renamed HAVSKJELL. *1959:* Owners became A/S Shellbatene, Norway. *1963:* Lengthened. *1972:* Sold to Shell Co. of Nigeria Ltd., Nigeria and renamed NIGERIA SHELL II. *1975:* Sold to National Oil Marketing Co., Nigeria and renamed NATIONAL EAGLE 2. *1978:* Sold for breaking up in Nigeria.

## M30. EMPIRE DEMON 1943-1946 Warrior class tug

O.N. 169110. 269g. 107.8 x 26.2 x 12.5 feet.

T.3-cyl. steam engine by North Eastern Marine Engineering Co. (1938) Ltd., Sunderland.

*31.12.1942:* Launched by J. Crown & Sons Ltd., Sunderland (Yard No. 207) for the Ministry of War Transport (C. Rowbotham & Sons, managers), London. *15.3.1943:* Completed. *15.3.1943-2.4.1949:* Taken over by the Admiralty for naval salvage duties. *1.4.1946:* Owners became the Ministry of Transport. *1946:* Managers became Risdon Beazley Ltd., Southampton. *2.4.1949:* Transferred permanently to the Admiralty. *26.3.1965:* While on voyage charter to the Londonderry Port and Harbour Commissioners, collided with NORSE LION (No, 12305g/53) while manoeuvring her in Lough Foyle. Taken out of service she went to Belfast for dry docking and surveys. Declared a constructive total loss. *1966:* Sold to Haulbowline Industries Ltd., Irish Republic for breaking up. *17.2.1966:* While sheltering off Ballymoney Bay, County Wexford, with DREDGER No. 2 (Br, 213g/30) which she was towing, the dredger was set adrift by heavy seas, grounded and became a total loss. The tug put into Dublin for stores and the crew deserted. *1966:* Resold to Hammond Lane Metal Co., Irish Republic. *14.3.1966:* Demolition commenced in Dublin.

## M31. EMPIRE MASCOT 1943-1946 Birch class tug

O.N. 169280. 244g. 106.7 x 26.7 x 11.6 feet.

T.3-cyl. steam engine by C.D. Holmes & Co. Ltd., Hull.

*9.3.1943:* Launched by Henry Scarr Ltd., Hessle (Yard No. S430) for the Ministry of War Transport (C. Rowbotham & Sons, managers), London. *19.5.1943:* Completed. *19.5.1943-21.7.1946:* In use on naval duties. *1.4.1946:* Owners became the Ministry of Transport. *27.7.1946:* Sold to Metal Industries Ltd. (T. McKenzie, manager), Glasgow. *1947:* Managers became Metal Industries (Salvage) Ltd. and renamed METINDA IV. *1948:* Sold to Alexandra Towing Co. Ltd., Liverpool. *1949:* Renamed FLYING KESTREL. *1969:* Sold to Haulbowline Industries Ltd., Irish Republic. *18.3.1969:* Arrived at Passage West in tow of MUMBLES (Br, 291g/69) for breaking up.

### M32. MANNINGTON 1943-1945

O.N. 168495. 1127g, 742n. 209.7 x 37.0 x 13.2 feet.

5-cyl. 2SA oil engine by Fairbanks, Morse & Co., Beloit, Wis.

*3.6.1942:* Launched by Barnes-Duluth Shipbuilding Co., Duluth, Minnesota (Yard No. 3) for the War Shipping Administration, United States of America. *5.1943:* Completed. *1943:* Placed on bareboat charter to the Ministry of War Transport (C. Rowbotham & Sons, managers), London. *25.5.1943-30.4.1945:* In use as a tanker on coastal and short sea duties. *1.5.1945:* Managers became Anglo-Saxon Petroleum Co. Ltd., London. *1.5.1945-26.9.1946:* In use as a tanker. *1946:* Returned to the U.S.A. *1946:* Sold to China Merchants Steam Navigation Co., China and renamed YUNG SIANG (Oil No. 127). *1947:* Sold to China Tanker Co. Ltd., China. *1949:* Taken over by the Republic of China (China People's Steam Navigation Company). *1961:* Owners became China Ocean Shipping Co. Continued existence in doubt.

MANNINGTON WSPL

### M33. SALT CREEK 1943-1945

O.N. 169610. 1127g, 740n. 209.7 x 37.0 x 13.2 feet.

5-cyl. 2SA oil engine by Fairbanks, Morse & Co., Beloit, Wis.

*3.7.1942:* Launched by Barnes-Duluth Shipbuilding Co., Duluth, Minnesota (Yard No. 4) for the War Shipping Administration, United States of America. *7.1943:* Completed. *1943:* Placed on bareboat charter to the Ministry of War Transport (C. Rowbotham & Sons, managers), London. *22.7.1943-30.4.1945:* In use as a tanker on coastal and short sea duties. *1.5.1945:* Managers became Anglo-Saxon Petroleum Co. Ltd., London. *1.5.1945-10.5.1946:* In use as a tanker. *1946:* Returned to the U.S.A. *1946:* Sold to the Argentinian Navy and renamed PUNTA RASA. *1970:* Sold to Gotaas-Larsen Argentina S.A., Argentina and renamed GAUCHITO. *1975:* Sold to Francisco Sgarra S.A., Argentina. After *1989* no further reference. Continued existence in doubt.

## M34. TONKAWA 1943-1945

O.N. 169630. 1124g, 736n. 209.7 x 37.0 x 13.2 feet.

5-cyl. 2SA oil engine by Fairbanks, Morse & Co., Beloit, Wis.

*26.8.1942:* Launched by Barnes-Duluth Shipbuilding Co., Duluth, Minnesota (Yard No. 7) for the War Shipping Administration, United States of America. *8.1943:* Completed. *1943:* Placed on bareboat charter to the Ministry of War Transport (C. Rowbotham & Sons, managers), London. *28.8.1943-10.1944:* In use as a tanker. *10.1944-7.9.1946:* In use as a water carrier. *1945:* Managers became Anglo-Saxon Petroleum Co. Ltd., London. *1946:* Returned to the U.S.A. *1946:* Sold to China Merchants Steam Navigation Co., China and renamed YUNG LUAN (Oil No. 124). *1947:* Sold to China Tanker Co. (China Merchants Steam Navigation Co. Ltd., managers), China. *1949:* Registry transferred to Formosa (Taiwan). *1965:* Broken up in Taiwan.


## M35. LOMA NOVIA 1943-1945

O.N. 169663. 1124g, 736n. 209.7 x 37.0 x 13.2 feet.

5-cyl. 2SA oil engine by Fairbanks, Morse & Co., Beloit, Wis.

*28.4.1943:* Launched by Barnes-Duluth Shipbuilding Co., Duluth, Minnesota (Yard No. 12) for the War Shipping Administration, United States of America. *10.1943:* Completed. *1943:* Placed on bareboat charter to the Ministry of War Transport (C. Rowbotham & Sons, managers), London. *30.9.1943-11.7.1946:* In use as a tanker. *1945:* Managers became Anglo-Saxon Petroleum Co. Ltd., London. *1946:* Returned to the U.S.A. *1946:* Sold to China Merchants Steam Navigation Co., China and renamed YUNG FU (Oil No. 121). *1947:* Sold to China Tanker Co. Ltd. (China Merchants Steam Navigation Co. Ltd., managers), China. *1949:* Registry transferred to Formosa (Taiwan). *2.1962:* Broken up at Keelung, Formosa.


## M36. SAXET 1943-1945

O.N. 169732. 1168g, 704n. 213.8 x 37.1 x 14.3 feet.

8-cyl. 4SA oil engine by Union Diesel Engineering Co., Oakland, California.

*20.12.1942:* Launched by Gray's Iron Works Inc., Galveston, Texas (Yard No. 102) for the War Shipping Administration, United States of America. *11.1943:* Completed. *1943:* Placed on bareboat charter to the Ministry of War Transport (C. Rowbotham & Sons, managers), London. *20.10.1943-26.9.1946:* In use as a tanker. *1945:* Managers became Anglo-Saxon Petroleum Co. Ltd., London. *1946:* Returned to the U.S.A. *1946:* Sold to China Merchants Steam Navigation Co., China and renamed YUNG SHU (Oil No. 113). *1947:* Sold to China Tanker Co. (China Merchants Steam Navigation Co. Ltd., managers), China. *1949:* Taken over by the Republic of China (China People's Steam Navigation Company). *1961:* Owners became China Ocean Shipping Co. Continued existence in doubt.

## M37. SULPHUR BLUFF 1944-1945

O.N. 169872. 1127g, 648n. 213.8 x 37.1 x 14.3 feet.

8-cyl. 4SA oil engine by National Supply Co., Springfield.

*21.8.1943:* Launched by Gray's Iron Works Inc., Galveston, Texas (Yard No. 107) for the War Shipping Administration, United States of America. *12.1943:* Completed. *1944:* Placed on bareboat charter to the Ministry of War Transport (C. Rowbotham & Sons, managers), London. *28.3.1944-24.4.1946:* In use as a tanker. *1945:* Managers became Anglo-Saxon Petroleum Co. Ltd., London. *1946:* Returned to the U.S.A. *1947:* Sold to the Argentinian Navy and renamed PUNTA CIGUENA. *7.2.1960:* Caught fire and sank in the River Urugany while on passage in ballast from Concepcion to Buenos Aires. Subsequently salvaged but details unknown. *1970:* Sold to Sarthou S.A., Argentina and renamed DONA ISABEL. After *1984* no further reference. Continued existence in doubt.


## M38. CHANT 23 1944-1946

O.N. 180108. 402g, 215n. 142.1 x 27.1 x 8.4 feet.

4-cyl. 2SA Crossley oil engine by Crossley Brothers Ltd., Manchester.

*10.2.1944:* Launched by Goole Shipbuilding & Repairing Co. Ltd., Goole (Yard No. 411) for the Ministry of War Transport (C. Rowbotham & Sons, managers), London. *29.2.1944:* Completed. *29.2.1944-25.9.1944:* In use as a tanker. *20.6.1944:* Beached on Normandy coast during gale, refloated and towed to Sheerness. *26.9.1944-29.7.1945:* In use as a water carrier. *30.7.1945-4.7.1946:* In use as a tanker. *1.4.1946:* Owners became the Ministry of Transport. *1946:* Sold to Algot Johansson and registered under the ownership of Rederi A/B Sally (Algot Johansson, managers), Finland and renamed SANNY. *1954:* Sold to Necati Pehlivan, Turkey and renamed NECATI PEHLIVAN II. *26.9.1954:* Stranded and sunk west of Lagskar after leaving Mariehamn, Finland, in ballast on delivery voyage to Istanbul.


## M39. CHANT 25 1944-1946

O.N. 180110. 402g, 215n. 142.1 x 27.1 x 8.4 feet.
From *1965:* 398g, 184n, 730d. 181.5 x 27.1 x 9.2 feet.

4-cyl. 2SA Crossley oil engine by Crossley Brothers Ltd., Manchester.
From *1957:* 4-cyl. 2SA oil engine by Skandiaverken A/B, Lysekil.
From *1967:* 6-cyl. 4SA oil engine by Ansaldo S.p.A., Stabilimento Meccanico, Genoa.

*13.3.1944:* Launched by Goole Shipbuilding & Repairing Co. Ltd., Goole (Yard No. 413) for the Ministry of War Transport (C. Rowbotham & Sons, managers), London. *27.3.1944:* Completed. *27.3.1944-23.7.1946:* In use as a tanker. *1.4.1946:* Owners became the Ministry of Transport. *1946:* Sold to Tronn Toenneberg, resold to A/S Troja Skipsrederi (Gunnar Jakonsen, managers), Norway and renamed RAKKE. *1951:* Sold to Lennart B. Kristensson & others, Sweden and renamed PORJUS. *1957:* Re-engined. *1963:* Sold to "Teulada" Societa Per Azioni di Navigazione, Italy and renamed CEDRINO. *1965:* Sold to Chiavari di Armamento, Italy, lengthened and renamed COMANDANTE UGO C. *1967:* Sold to Compagnia Armatoriale Siculo Adriatica (C.A.S.A.) S.p.A., Italy, re-engined and renamed NONNO GIGI. *27.11.1969* and *3.12.1969:* Severely damaged in heavy weather and put back to Genoa. Declared a constructive total loss. *1971:* Sold to Messrs. Lotti S.p.A., Italy for breaking up. *6.1971:* Demolition commenced at yard of Ditta Lotti, La Spezia.

**M40. Y-22** 1944

494g, 287n, 747d.   155.2 x 27.1 x 12.9 feet.

6-cyl. 4SA oil engine by Enterprise Engine & Foundry Co., San Francisco.

*8.1943:* Completed by Levingston Shipbuilding Co., Orange, Texas (Yard No. 268) for U.S. Army Transportation Corps. *1944:* Managers became C. Rowbotham & Sons. *1948/9:* Sold to Le Quellec & Compagnie, Morocco, used as a wine tanker and renamed PHRYN. *1961/2:* Converted into a wine tanker. *1965:* Sold to Société Maritime (H. Lary & Compagnie), France and renamed MACTA. *1968:* Sold to Spirit Shipping & Transports Co., Greece and renamed ELPIDA 1. *1972:* Sold to Ktimatonaftiliaki S.A., Greece and renamed ELIANA. *1980:* Sold to Nafs Shipping Co., Greece and renamed EDDA. *17.4.1983:* While on passage between Perama and Mitylene in heavy weather sustained engine trouble off Mitylene Island. Towed to Perama for repairs. *1.6.1983:* Returned to service. *31.10.1984:* Arrived Eleusis, Greece, to be broken up by Sotiropoulos Brothers & Co. *12.1984:* Demolition commenced.


**M41. Y-23** 1944

484g, 358n, 700d.   155.2 x 27.1 x 12.9 feet.

6-cyl. 4SA oil engine by Enterprise Engine & Foundry Co., San Francisco.

*9.1943:* Completed by Equitable Equipment Co. Inc., Madisonville (Yard No. 193) for the U.S. Army Transportation Corps. *1944:* Managers became C. Rowbotham & Sons. *1948:* Sold to Compañia Maritima Caralaga, Honduras and renamed CARMEN. *1951/2:* Sold to Société Frêt Maroc, Morocco. *1955:* Sold to K. Diamantis, Greece and renamed FRYNI. *1959:* Transferred to Greek Tankershipping Co. Ltd., Greece, and subsequently renamed YIANNAKIS S.1982:* Sold to Nafs Shipping Co., Greece and renamed TAKIS V. *1984:* Renamed RODINI. Continued existence in doubt.


**M42. CHANT 27** 1944-1946

O.N. 180112.   402g, 215n.   142.2 x 27.0 x 8.5 feet.

4-cyl. 2SA Crossley oil engine by Crossley Brothers Ltd., Manchester.
From *2.1969:* 6-cyl. 2SA Newbury oil engine by Newbury Diesel Co. Ltd., Newbury.

*26.4.1944:* Launched by Goole Shipbuilding & Repairing Co. Ltd., Goole (Yard No. 415) for the Ministry of War Transport (C. Rowbotham & Sons, managers), London. *4.5.1944:* Completed. *4.5.1944-18.7.1946:* In use as a tanker. *1.4.1946:* Owners became the Ministry of Transport. *1946:* Sold to John Catapodis, resold to La Sociedade de Navegacion Comagre S.A. (Neill & Pandelis Ltd., managers), Panama. *1947:* Renamed COMAGRE. *1947:* Sold to N.V. Teerbedrijf Uithoorn, Netherlands and renamed FRANS. *1954:* Sold to N.V. Rederij "Frans", Netherlands. *1955:* Sold to F.T. Everard & Sons Ltd., London and renamed AUSPICITY. *2.1969:* Re-engined. *1972:* Sold to Panagiotis Vourdahas & Associates, Greece and renamed THEKLI. *1973:* Presumed broken up in Piraeus, Greece.

## M43. CHANT 11 1944-1945

Cf. Owned Ships No. 20 LEADSMAN

## M44. EMPIRE ROSEBERY 1944

O.N. 169412. 2370g, 1281n. 290.7 x 44.1 x 19.1 feet.

T.3-cyl. steam engine by D. Rowan & Co. Ltd., Glasgow.

*22.5.1944:* Launched by Blythswood Shipbuilding Co. Ltd., Glasgow (Yard No. 77) for the Ministry of War Transport (C. Rowbotham & Sons, managers), London. *5.7.1944:* Completed. *5.7.1944-24.8.1944:* In use as a tanker. *24.8.1944:* Mined and sunk while in ballast between Port en Bessin and the Hamble in position 49° 22'N, 00° 36'W with the loss of 10 crew and 3 gunners from a crew of 24 plus 8 gunners.

## M45. CHANT 12 1944-1945

O.N. 180267. 403g, 214n. 142.2 x 27.0 x 8.5 feet.

5-cyl. 4SA Ruston oil engine by Ruston & Hornsby Ltd., Lincoln.

*6.1944:* Launched by Henry Scarr Ltd., Hessle (Yard No. 446) for the Ministry of War Transport (C. Rowbotham & Sons, managers), London. *10.7.1944:* Completed. *10.7.1944-3.9.1944:* In use as a tanker. *4.9.1944-25.11.1945:* In use as a water carrier. *1945:* Sold to the French Government. *1946:* Sold to Port Autonome de Havre, France. *1957:* Sold to Société Maritime de Degazage, France and renamed S.M.D. 1. *1974:* Sold to B.V. Vacuum Cleaning, Netherlands, converted into a tanker cleaning vessel and renamed SUCCESS III. Still in service in Rotterdam.

## M46. EMPIRE BARKIS 1944-1946

O.N. 169940. 340g, 139n. 146.8 x 23.7 x 9.3 feet.

4-cyl. 2SA oil engine by British Auxiliaries Ltd., Glasgow.

*8.6.1944:* Launched by Rowhedge Ironworks Co. Ltd., Rowhedge (Yard No. 639) for the Ministry of War Transport (C. Rowbotham & Sons, managers), London. *1.9.1944:* Completed. *1.9.1944-1.2.1946:* In use as a tanker in coastal and short sea trade. *1946:* Sold to Van Castricum & Co. Ltd., Sanderstead, Surrey and renamed SODOK. *1947:* Sold to Shell Co. of Singapore Ltd., Singapore and renamed GUNTUR. *1961:* Sold to Union Boatyard, Singapore. *1962:* Sold to Madam Dolly Seal, Singapore. *1971:* Sold to P.T. Perusahaan Pelajaran Nusantara "Palka Utama", Indonesia. Continued existence in doubt.

## M47. EMPIRE BOXER 1944-1946

Cf. Owned Ships No. 17 CHARTSMAN

**M48. EMPIRE FOLK** 1944-1945 Maple class tug

O.N. 168782. 129g. 92.5 x 20.5 x 8.4 feet.

T.3-cyl. steam engine by McKie & Baxter Ltd., Paisley.

*18.3.1942:* Launched by R. Dunston Ltd., Thorne (Yard No. T365) for the Ministry of War Transport (Pedder & Mylchreest Ltd., managers), London. *13.5.1942:* Completed. *13.5.1942-22.3.1944:* In use on naval duties. *1944:* Managers became C. Rowbotham & Sons. *23.3.1944-10.6.1944:* In use on coastal towing duties. *11.6.1944:* Transferred to naval duties. *1945:* Managers became Ponts et Chaussees, France. *1.4.1946*: Owners became the Ministry of Transport. *6.1947:* Sold to the French Government. *1947:* Sold to Chambre de Commerce Dieppe, France. *1950:* Renamed JEHAN DE BETHANCOURT. *1951:* Owners became Chambre de Commerce de Dieppe. *1962:* Owners became Chambre de Commerce et d'Industrie de Dieppe. *1969:* Sold to Jean Thommerel, France for breaking up. *4.1970:* Demolition commenced at Fecamp.


**M49. Y-31** 1944

484g, 310n, 715d. 157.4 x 27.1 x 12.6 feet.

6-cyl. 4SA oil engine by Enterprise Engine & Foundry Co., San Francisco.

*3.1944:* Completed by Kyle & Co. Inc., Stockton, California (Yard No. 18) for the U.S. Army Transportation Corps. *1944:* Managers became C. Rowbotham & Sons. *1946:* Sold to Skibs A/S av 1918 (A/S Rederiet Odfjell, managers), Norway and renamed LONN. *1947:* Sold to Sigurd Soreng Rederi A/S, Norway. *1948:* Sold to A/S Marly (Paul Blich, manager), Norway and renamed LITEN. *1950:* Manager became Reidar Wahl. *1955:* Sold to The Monrovia Navigation Co. Inc., Liberia and renamed MABULI. *1961:* Sold to Farrell Lines Inc., Liberia for coasting feeder service in Liberia. *1970:* Sold to Zarate & Martinez, Spain. Continued existence in doubt.


**M50. Y-32** 1944

484g, 310n, 715d. 155.8 x 27.1 x 12.5 feet.

6-cyl. 4SA oil engine by Enterprise Engine & Foundry Co., San Francisco.

*4.1944:* Completed by Kyle & Co. Inc., Stockton, California (Yard No. 19) for the U.S. Army Transportation Corps. *1944:* Managers became C. Rowbotham & Sons. *1947:* Sold to Compañia de Navegacion Alencia S.A., Panama, registered in Honduras and renamed ANA. *1952:* Sold to Empresa Moraes de Navegacao Costeira S.A., Brazil and renamed JOSIAS-MORAES. *1979:* Lloyd's Register amends name to JOSIAS DE MORAES. *1982:* Sold to Global Transporte Oceanico S.A., Brazil. Continued existence in doubt.

### M51. Y-40 1944

630g.   183.4 x 30.0 x 12.0 feet.

2 6-cyl. 2SA oil engines by Fairbanks, Morse & Co., Beloit.

*10/11.1943:* Completed by Odenbach Shipbuilding Corporation, Rochester, New York (Yard No. 15) for the U.S. Army Transportation Corps. *1944:* Managers became C. Rowbotham & Sons. *1947:* Sold to Société Frêt Maroc, Morocco, converted into a wine tanker and renamed CAROLA. *1950:* Renamed TAMELELT. *c.1952:* Sold to Société Navale de l'Atlantique, Morocco. *1957:* Sold to Alessandro Cinciari S.p.A., Italy and renamed LISA C. *1963:* Sold to Societe Imprese Marittime e Navigazione S.p.A., Italy and renamed ALICUDI. Converted into an oil tanker. *1975:* Sold to Sarda Bunkers S.p.A., Italy. Believed to be still in existence.

ALICUDI, ex Y-40 at Naples on 26th September 1968          Wm. A. Schell

### M52. Y-78 1944

632g, 334n, 1015d.   178.6 x 30.1 x 12.0 feet.

2 4-cyl. 2SA oil engines by Clark Brothers Co., Cleveland, Ohio.

*6.1944:* Completed by Odenbach Shipbuilding Corporation, Rochester, New York (Yard No. 28) for the U.S. Army Transportation Corps. *1944:* Managers became C. Rowbotham & Sons. *2.1947:* Sold to Navegacao e Comercio Sergipe-Parana S.A., Brazil, converted into a dry cargo vessel by Marine Basin Co., Brooklyn, New York and renamed HELIUS. *1952:* Sold to Azevedo & Cia. Ltda., Brazil and renamed URUBATAN. *9.4.1959:* Exploded and caught fire at Ilheus inner harbour with a cargo of asphalt. Wreck beached and declared a constructive total loss.

**M53. Y-82** 1944

632g, 334n, 1015d.   179.3 x 30.0 x 12.0 feet.

2 4-cyl. 2SA oil engines by Clark Brothers Co., Cleveland.

*7.1944:* Completed by Odenbach Shipbuilding Corporation, Rochester, New York (Yard No. 32) for the U.S. Army Transportation Corps. *1944:* Managers became C. Rowbotham & Sons. *3.1947:* Sold to N.V. Nederlandsch-Indische Tankstoomboot Maatschappij, Netherlands, converted into a dry cargo vessel and renamed BETOERAN. *1949:* Owners became N.V. Nederlands-Indonesische Tankvaart Maatschappij, Indonesia. *1956:* Sold to Lancey Steamships Pty. Ltd., Australia and renamed BASS POINT. *1964:* Owners became Lancey Shipping New Guinea Pty. Ltd., Papua New Guinea and renamed NEW GUINEA TRADER. *1965:* Sold to Mutual Rights Steamship Co. Ltd., Hong Kong. *1966:* Sold to Rabia & United Associates Ltd., Hong Kong. *1968:* Sold to Trung Nam Hang Hai Cong Ty, Vietnam and renamed DONG HAI. Owners became the Government of The Socialist Republic of Vietnam. Continued existence in doubt.

**M54. Y-83** 1944

632g, 334n, 1015d.   179.4 x 30.0 x 13.5 feet.

2 4-cyl. 2SA oil engines by Clark Brothers Co., Cleveland.
From *1970:* 2 6-cyl. 4SA oil engines by Skoda, Prague.

*7.1944:* Completed by Odenbach Shipbuilding Corporation, Rochester, New York (Yard No. 33) for the U.S. Army Transportation Corps. *1944:* Managers became C. Rowbotham & Sons. *1948:* Sold to Compañia Maritima Tarralona S.A., Panama and renamed TINA, with registry transferred to Honduras. *1951:* Sold to Frêt-Tunis (Compagnie d'Armement de Navires-Citernes, managers), Tunis, with registry transferred to France. *1953:* Sold to Société Frêt-Maroc, Morocco and converted into a butane tanker. *1957:* Sold to Compagnie d'Armement Maritime S.A., Djibouti and renamed AMBADO. *1962:* Sold to Stella Maritime & Trading Corporation (Michel C. Xydia, manager), Greece and renamed MEDGAS. *1970:* Sold to E.C. Babounis, Greece, converted into a liquefied gas tanker, re-engined and renamed MEDGAS II. Still afloat in *1983.*

**M55. Y-104** 1944

639g, 335n, 1015d.   178.4 x 30.1 x 12.0 feet.

2 6-cyl. 4SA oil engines by Wolverine Motor Works, Inc.

*8.1944:* Completed by Kane Shipbuilding Corporation, Galveston, Texas (Yard No. 4) for the U.S. Army Transportation Corps. *1944:* Managers became C. Rowbotham & Sons. *1948:* Sold to unspecified owners, Panama and renamed ALEXANDRIA. *1948:* Sold to Société d'Armement de Navires Citernes (SANC), Morocco and renamed MAROCAIN. *1949:* Renamed MERIEM. *1952:* Believed sold to French Government agency and renamed LIEUTENANT PAULL MARCK. *1959:* Sold to "Anapo" Compagnia di Navigazione e Bunkeraggi S.p.A., Italy and renamed ORITIGIA. *1967:* Owners became Ciane-Anapa Compagnia de Navigazione e Bunkeraggi S.p.A., Italy. *12.1984:* Sold to Ditta Riccardi for breaking up at Vado Ligure, Italy.

### M56. EMPIRE ORKNEY 1945-1946

O.N. 169433. 813g, 334n. 193.0 x 30.7 x 13.8 feet.

T.3-cyl. steam engine by Aitchison, Blair Ltd., Clydebank.

*30.11.1944:* Launched by A. & J. Inglis Ltd., Glasgow (Yard No. 1287) for the Ministry of War Transport (C. Rowbotham & Sons, managers), London. *26.2.1945:* Completed. *26.2.1945-11.10.1945:* In use as a tanker. *12.10.1945-22.8.1946:* In use as a water carrier. *1.4.1946:* Owners became the Ministry of Transport and managers became Tankers Transit & Shipping Co. Ltd., London. *1949:* Sold to F.T. Everard & Sons Ltd., London and renamed ALCHYMIST. *1969:* Sold to Brugse Scheepsloperij, Belgium. *3.5.1969:* Arrived at Bruges for breaking up.

### M57. EMPIRE ANGLESEY 1945-1946

O.N. 180382. 288g, 104n. 136.4 x 21.5 x 8.5 feet.

6-cyl. 2SA Crossley oil engine by Crossley Brothers Ltd., Manchester.

*16.6.1945:* Launched by J. Harker Ltd., Knottingley (Yard No. 169) for the Ministry of War Transport (C. Rowbotham & Sons, managers), London. *10.1945:* Completed. *10.1945-12.11.1945:* In use as a tanker on coastal and short sea duties. *1.4.1946:* Owners became the Ministry of Transport. *21.8.1946:* Sold to A/S Tankskibsrederiet (K.V. Tersling, managers), Denmark and renamed ABADAN. *1961:* Sold to Celtic Coasters Ltd., Irish Republic and renamed RENEE J. *1969:* Sold for breaking up in the Irish Republic.

EMPIRE NICKLEBY                    Welsh Industrial & Maritime Museum

## M58. EMPIRE NICKLEBY 1945-1946

O.N. 181012. 306g, 107n. 127.2 x 24.1 x 10.3 feet.

6-cyl. 2SA oil engine by British Auxiliaries Ltd., Glasgow.

*17.7.1945:* Launched by I. Pimblott & Sons Ltd., Northwich (Yard No. 663) for the Ministry of War Transport (C. Rowbotham & Sons, managers), London. *11.12.1945:* Completed. *11.12.1945-1.10.1946:* In use as a tanker. *1.4.1946:* Owners became the Ministry of Transport. *1946:* Sold to Compania de Navegacion "Anne" S.A. (C. Rowbotham & Sons, managers), Panama and renamed NICKLEBY. *1947:* Sold to Compania di Navegacion Teresita S.A. (Fratelli Cosulich, managers), Panama. *1950:* Sold to Bombay (later renamed Mumbai) Port Trust, India, converted into a water tanker and renamed NIRMALA. Still in service.

## M59. EMPIRE STICKLEBACK 1945-1946

O.N. 131060. 1984g, 1447n. 247.6 x 40.1 x 23.4 feet.

T.3-cyl. steam engine by Frontier Iron Works, Detroit.

*1895:* Completed by Chicago Shipbuilding Co., Chicago for Minnesota Steamship Co. (Pickands, Mather & Co., managers), United States of America as the steel barge MALTA. *1901:* Sold to Pittsburgh Steamship Co., United States of America. *1912:* Sold to Canadian Towing & Wrecking Co. (J. Whalen, manager), United States of America. *1913:* Sold to J. Whalen, Ontario, Canada and renamed THUNDER BAY. *1915:* Sold to Canadian North West Steamship Co. Ltd. (W.L. Reed, manager), Canada. *1917:* Sold to Montreal Transportation Co. Ltd., Canada. *1918:* Sold to H.B. Smith, Havana, Cuba. *1920:* Registry transferred to Canada. *1921:* Sold to Canada Steamship Lines Ltd., Canada and rebuilt by Davie Shipbuilding & Repairing Co., Lauzon, Province of Quebec, as a steam general cargo ship. *14.12.1922:* Went ashore at Morgan's Point on Lake Erie while carrying a cargo of grain. *25.12.1922:* Refloated and taken to Port Colborne before proceeding to Buffalo for repairs. *1940:* Sold to Branch Lines Ltd., Canada, converted into an oil tanker and renamed PINEBRANCH. *1944:* Sold to the Ministry of War Transport (Anglo-American Oil Co. Ltd., managers), London. *2.12.1944-28.5.1946:* In use as a tanker. *1945:* Managers became C. Rowbotham & Sons and renamed EMPIRE STICKLEBACK. *1946:* Sold to Branch Lines Ltd. (Marine Industries Ltd., managers), Canada and renamed PINEBRANCH. *1954/5:* Laid up. *1961:* Dismantled and sunk for use as a wharf.

## M60. EXCALIBUR 1945-1946 Tug

O.N. 180766. 143g. 95.0 x 21.6 x 9.8 feet.

T.3-cyl. steam engine by A.G. "Weser", Bremen.

*21.12.1920:* Launched by A.G. "Weser", Bremen (Yard No. 387) for Lutgens & Reimers, Germany as FINKENWARDER. *1945:* Handed over to the Ministry of War Transport (C. Rowbotham & Sons, managers), London and renamed EXCALIBUR. *1.2.1945-7.6.1946:* In use on miscellaneous naval duties. *1.4.1946:* Owners became the Ministry of Transport. *6.1946:* Transferred to the U.S.S.R. by the Tripartite Naval Commission. *1960:* Deleted from Lloyd's Register.

## M61. EXPONENT 1945-1950 Tug

O.N. 181161.   139g.   89.9 x 21.6 x 11.1 feet.

C.4-cyl. steam engine by  Christiansen & Meyer, Hamburg.

*2.11.1937:* Launched by Joh. Oelkers, Hamburg (Yard No. 486) for Petersen & Alpers, Germany as JAN. *1945:* Handed over to the Ministry of War Transport (C. Rowbotham & Sons, managers), London and renamed EXPONENT. *20.11.1945-18.2.1946:* In use on port duties. *1.4.1946:* Owners became the Ministry of Transport. *1950:* Sold to Services des Ports et Chausses, France. *1965:* Sold to Port Autonome de Nantes, France. Fate unknown.


## M62. EXUBERANT 1945-1946 Tug

O.N. 180786.   172g, 27n.   80.0 x 22.7 x 9.3 feet.

C.4-cyl. steam engine by Christiansen & Meyer, Hamburg.

*2.3.1944:* Launched by Joh. Oelkers, Hamburg (Yard No. 508) for Lutgens & Reimers, Germany as SCHULAU. *11.1944:* Completed. *1945:* Handed over to the Ministry of War Transport (C. Rowbotham & Sons, managers), London and renamed EXUBERANT. *15.10.1945-12.12.1945:* Not allocated. *16.12.1945-31.5.1946:* In use on miscellaneous naval duties. *1.4.1946:* Owners became the Ministry of Transport. *5.1946:* Transferred to the U.S.S.R. by the Tripartite Naval Commission. *1970:* Deleted from Lloyd's Register.


## M63. EMPIRE TIGLAS 1945 800g.

*1942:* Completed in Germany for German owners as DANISCH WOHLD. *13.10.1945:* Handed over to the Ministry of War Transport (C. Rowbotham & Sons, managers), London and allocated the name EMPIRE TIGLAS. *15-22.10.1945:* In use as a tanker. *23.10.1945:* Bareboat chartered to the Government of the Netherlands (N.V. Phs. Van Ommeren's Scheepvaartbedrijf, managers), converted to a lighter and renamed ELST. Fate unknown.


## M64. EMPIRE TEGENYA 1945-1946

902g, 565n.   206.2 x 36.6 x 12.5 feet.
From *1934:* 1172g, 794n, 1783d.   244.7 x 36.6 x 15.8 feet.

2 6-cyl. 4SA oil engines by Maschinenfabrik Augsburg-Nurnberg A.G., Augsburg.

*12.11.1930:* Launched by Deutsche Werft A.G., Hamburg (Yard No. 147) for Atlantic-Tank-Rhederei G.m.b.H. (John T. Essberger G.m.b.H., managers), Germany as ELSA ESSBERGER. *12.1930:* Completed. *1934:* Lengthened. *1936:* Owners became John T. Essberger. *1938:* Renamed LISA ESSBERGER. *3.9.1945:* Handed over to the Ministry of War Transport (C. Rowbotham & Sons, managers), London and allocated the name EMPIRE TEGENYA. Laid up. *1.4.1946:* Owners became the Ministry of Transport. *11.8.1946:* Returned to German owners and renamed LISA ESSBERGER. *1960/1:* Sold to Carl Robert Eckelmann, Federal Republic of Germany. *1973:* Still in service. Fate unknown.

EMPIRE DARBY                                    National Maritime Museum

## M65. EMPIRE DARBY 1946 Modified Hornby class tug

O.N. 169083. 203g. 95.2 x 25.1 x 12.4 feet.

T.3-cyl. steam engine by McKie & Baxter Ltd., Paisley.
From *1962:* 16-cyl. 2SA vee oil engine by General Motors Corporation, Cleveland, Ohio.

*8.1.1943:* Launched by Cochrane & Sons Ltd., Selby (Yard No. 1261) for the Ministry of War Transport (London, Midland & Scottish Railway Co., managers), London. *20.4.1943:* Completed. *20.4.1943-5.1944:* In use on naval duties. *4.1944:* Managers became Alexandra Towing Co. Ltd., Liverpool. *5.1944-18.5.1944:* In use on coastal towing duties. *19.5.1944-6.2.1946:* In use on naval duties. *10.1945:* Managers became Overseas Towage & Salvage Co. Ltd., London. *7.2.1946-30.5.1947:* In use on port duties. *1.4.1946:* Owners became the Ministry of Transport and managers became C. Rowbotham & Sons. *1946:* Managers became Overseas Towage & Salvage Co. Ltd., London. *31.5.1947:* Taken over permanently by the Admiralty for naval duties and renamed EGERTON. *29.7.1958:* Sold to H.G. Pounds, Portsmouth. *1961:* Sold to J.D. Irving Ltd., Canada and renamed IRVING BEECH. *1962:* Re-engined. *1.12.1967:* Grounded near New Waterford at the mouth of Sydney Harbour, Nova Scotia, following a generator failure, while towing the motor tanker LUBROLAKE (Ca, 1622g/37) and a barge. All three went ashore and were abandoned.

EMPIRE IMP                                    Andrew Huckett Collection

## M66. EMPIRE IMP 1946 Maple class tug

O.N. 168785.   129g.   92.5 x 20.5 x 8.4 feet.

T.3-cyl. steam engine by Worsley Mesnes Ironworks Ltd., Wigan.

*22.5.1942:* Launched by R. Dunston Ltd., Thorne (Yard No. T375) for the Ministry of War Transport (Overseas Towage & Salvage Co. Ltd., managers), London. *3.7.1942:* Completed. *3.7.1942-5.1.1945:* In use on naval duties. *1.8.1942:* Took list and capsized alongside jetty at Pembroke Dock. *22.8.1942:* Refloated and taken to a berth at Milford for repairs. *20.1.1945-30.5.1945:* In

EMPIRE IMP                                                              WSS

use on coastal towing duties with Clyde Shipping Co. Ltd., Glasgow as managers. *31.5.1945-4.1946:* In use on salvage operations with Liverpool & Glasgow Association as managers. *4.1946-28.7.1946:* Taken over by the Admiralty for naval port duties with C. Rowbotham & Sons as managers. *29.7.1946-14.8.1946:* Not allocated. *15.8.1946-30.10.1959:* In use on naval duties at Harwich and Sheerness. *30.10.1959:* Laid up at Chatham. *8.1960:* Sold to H.G. Pounds, Portsmouth. *1960:* Sold to J.D. Irving Ltd., Canada and renamed IRVING WALNUT. *3.1969:* Demolished to the waterline. *14.3.1969:* Hull scuttled at sea.

## M67. EMPIRE CEDAR  1946  Maple class tug

O.N. 168774.  129g.  92.5 x 20.5 x 8.4 feet.

T.3-cyl. steam engine by McKie & Baxter Ltd., Paisley.

*26.9.1941:* Launched by R. Dunston Ltd., Thorne (Yard No. T360) for the Ministry of War Transport (Ross & Marshall Ltd., Glasgow, managers), London. *12.11.1941:* Completed. *12.11.1941-12.12.1944:* In use on naval duties. *23.1.1945-15.4.1946:* On charter to the Belgian Government. *1.4.1946:* Owners became the Ministry of Transport. *16.4.1946-25.4.1946:* Redelivered by the Belgians. *25.4.1946-15.6.1946:* Laid up. *16.6.1946-9.1946:* In use on naval duties at Harwich with C. Rowbotham & Sons as managers. *9.1946:* Laid up. *31.10.1946:* Released from service, managers becoming Townsend Brothers Ferries Ltd., London. *24.1.1947:* Sold to United Towing Co. Ltd., Hull and renamed HANDYMAN. *27.4.1966:* Arrived at Bo'ness to be broken up by P. & W. MacLellan Ltd.

## M68. EMPIRE LUCY  1946/1951-1962  Birch class tug

O.N. 181261.  244g.  106.7 x 26.7 x 11.6 feet.

T.3-cyl. steam engine by George Fletcher & Co. Ltd., Derby.

*6.3.1946:* Launched by J.S. Watson (Gainsborough) Ltd., Gainsborough (Yard No. 1556) for the Ministry of War Transport (C. Rowbotham & Sons, managers), London. *1.4.1946:* Owners became the Ministry of Transport. *23.5.1946:* Completed. *23.5.1946:* Taken over by the Admiralty for naval duties at Harwich. *1951:* Managers became C. Rowbotham & Sons. *1956:* Managers became C. Rowbotham & Sons (Management) Ltd. *1958:* Released from service. *1958:* Owners became the Ministry of Transport & Civil Aviation. *1962:* Sold to Imprese Marittime Augustea S.p.A., Italy and renamed OGNINA. *1972:* Reported taken over by the Italian Navy. Fate unknown.

## C. ROWBOTHAM AND SONS
## ROWBOTHAM TANKSHIPS LTD.

## VESSELS MANAGED ON BEHALF OF OTHER OWNERS

### R1.  NICKLEBY 1946-1950

Managed on behalf of Compania de Navegacion "Anne" S.A.
Cf. Managed Vessels No. M58 EMPIRE NICKLEBY

### R2.  OSCO INGRAM OSPREY 1982-1987

O.N. 399093/L.R. 8009246.   18959g, 12811n, 29999d.
170,52(BB) x 27,03 x 10,264 metres.

6-cyl. 2SA B&W oil engine by J.G. Kincaid & Co. Ltd., Greenock.
11400bhp.   14,75k.

*2.11.1981:* Launched by Swan Hunter Shipbuilders Ltd., Wallsend & Neptune
Yards, Wallsend (Yard No. 114) for Ingram Tankships Ltd. & Tampimex Oil
Ltd. (Rowbotham Tankships Ltd., managers), London as INGRAM OSPREY.
*7.1982:* Completed as OSCO INGRAM OSPREY. *1984:* Renamed INGRAM
OSPREY. *1986:* Sold to Helmsman Tankships Ltd. (Rowbotham Tankships
Ltd., managers), London and renamed PETROBULK ROVER. *1987:* Sold to
Varun Shipping Co. Ltd., India and renamed VISHWADOOT. Still in service.

OSCO INGRAM OSPREY on sea trials on 23rd April 1982          Nigel J. Cutts

### R3.  IRISHGATE 1982-1993

Cf. P&O Tankships Ltd. Owned Ships No. P15.

IRISHGATE off Portishead on 22nd February 1998      Bernard McCall

## R4. PER 1982-1983

O.N. 121881/L.R. 8004088.   1100g, 679n, 1774d.
69,53 x 11,82 x 4,313 metres.

6-cyl. 4SA Yanmar oil engine by Yanmar Diesel Engine Co. Ltd., Amagasaki.
1400bhp.   10,5k.

*13.5.1980:* Launched by Fukuoka Zosen K.K., Fukuoka (Yard No. 1080) for
K.K. Nippo Unyu Shokai (Hull Gates Shipping Management Ltd., managers),
Japan. *8.1980:* Completed. *10.1982:* Managers became Rowbotham
Tankships Ltd. *9.1983:* Managers became Maritime Ship Management Ltd.
*1985:* Sold to North British Shipping Ltd., Hull and registry transferred to the
Bahamas. *1986:* Sold to Lloyds Leasing (North Sea Transport) Ltd. (Bowker
& King Ltd., managers), London and renamed BARMOUTH, retaining
Bahamas registry. *1989:* Managers became Crescent Shipping Ltd. *1997:*
Owners became Crescent Navigation Ltd. (Crescent Shipping Ltd.,
managers) and registry transferred to London. *1999:* Managers became
Crescent Marine Services Ltd. Still in service.

PER at Jersey on 5th August 1983      Dave Hocquard

### R5. CHRISTIAN 1982-1983

O.N. 121880/L.R. 8004090.   1098g, 678n, 1767d.
69,53 x 11,82 x 4,314 metres.

6-cyl. 4SA Yanmar oil engine by Yanmar Diesel Engine Co. Ltd., Amagasaki. 1400bhp.   10,5k.

*16.6.1980:* Launched by Fukuoka Zosen K.K., Fukuoka (Yard No. 1081) for K.K. Nippo Unyu Shokai (Hull Gates Shipping Management Ltd., managers), Japan. *10.1980:* Completed. *10.1982:* Managers became Rowbotham Tankships Ltd. *9.1983:* Managers became Maritime Ship Management Ltd. *1985:* Sold to Jewel Tank Ship S.A. (North British Shipping Ltd., managers), Panama and registered in the Bahamas. *1988:* Sold to F.T. Everard Shipping Ltd. (F.T. Everard & Sons Ltd., managers), London and renamed AMITY, retaining Bahamas registry. *2000:* Sold to Krabbeskars Rederi AB, Sweden and renamed SMARAGD. Still in service.

CHRISTIAN at Birkenhead on 11th December 1980           Dave Hocquard

### R6. STEN 1982-1983

O.N. 123754/L.R. 8021098.   1100g, 680n, 1763d.
69,53 x 11,82 x 4,314 metres.

6-cyl. 4SA Yanmar oil engine by Yanmar Diesel Engine Co. Ltd., Amagasaki. 1400bhp.   10,5k.

*18.11.1980:* Launched by Kitanihon Zosen K.K., Hachinoke (Yard No. 166) for K.K. Nippo Unyu Shokai (Hull Gates Shipping Management Ltd., managers), Japan. *2.1981:* Completed. *10.1982:* Managers became Rowbotham Tankships Ltd. *9.1983:* Managers became Maritime Ship Management Ltd. *1985:* Sold to Gemmer Tank Ship S.A. (North British Shipping Ltd., managers), Panama. *1986:* Sold to Lloyds Leasing (North Sea Transport) Ltd. (Bowker & King Ltd., managers), London and renamed BARDSEY. *1989:* Managers became Crescent Shipping Ltd. *1990:* Registry transferred to the Bahamas. *1990:* Managers became Crescent Shipping (France) S.a.r.l. and registry transferred to France. *1991:* Managers became Crescent Shipping Ltd. and registry transferred to the Bahamas. *1997:* Owners became Crescent Navigation Ltd. (Crescent Shipping Ltd., managers) and registry transferred to London. *1999:* Managers became Crescent Marine Services Ltd. Still in service.

STEN at Jersey on 17th May 1984                    Dave Hocquard

## R7.  NATALIE 1982-1983

O.N. 123773/L.R. 8024870.   1101g, 675n, 1777d.
69,53 x 11,82 x 4,314 metres.

6-cyl. 2SA Yanmar oil engine by Yanmar Diesel Engine Co. Ltd., Amagasaki.
1400bhp.   10,5k.

*9.2.1981:* Launched by Fukuoka Zosen K.K., Fukuoka (Yard No. 1087) for First
Maritime K.K. (Hull Gates Shipping Management Ltd., managers), Japan.
*4.1981:* Completed. *10.1982:* Managers became Rowbotham Tankships Ltd.
*9.1983:* Managers became Maritime Ship Management Ltd. *1985:* Sold to
Gemmar Tank Ship S.A. (Nippon Fleet Co. Ltd., managers), Panama. *6.1988:*
Sold to F.T. Everard Shipping Ltd. (F.T. Everard & Sons Ltd., managers),
London, registered in the Bahamas and renamed AVERITY. Still in service.

NATALIE berthing at Jersey on 15th July 1983           Dave Hocquard

**R8.  NORTHGATE** 1982-1993

Cf. P&O Tankships Ltd. Owned Ships No. P16.

**R9.  OSCO TAMPIMEX EAGLE** 1983-1984

O.N. 377168/L.R. 7389699.  18493g, 12657n, 32259d.
170,97(BB) x 25,94 x 11,361 metres.

7-cyl. 2SA oil engine by A/S Burmeister & Wain's Motor-og Maskinfabrik af 1971, Kobenhavn.  13100bhp.  15k.

*15.7.1976:* Launched by Gotaverken Finnboda AB, Stockholm (Yard No. 396) for Rautogate Ltd., London as NORDIC AURORA. *1.1977:* Completed for Nordic Aurura Shipping Ltd. (Wallem Shipmanagement (U.K.) Ltd., managers), London. *1979:* Sold to Tampimex Oil Ltd. (Wallem Shipmanagement (U.K.) Ltd., managers), London and renamed TAMPIMEX EAGLE. *1980:* Renamed OSCO TAMPIMEX EAGLE. *1983:* Sold to Ingram Tankships Ltd. & Tampimex Oil Ltd. (Rowbotham Tankships Ltd., managers), London. *1984:* Sold to Akropan Shipping Corporation, Bahamas and renamed SOUTHERN CROSS. *4.6.1986:* A serious explosion occurred while loading at Skikda, Algeria. The ship caught fire and was towed out of port. Three members of the crew were killed. Beached off Skikda and, on *12.6.1986*, broke in two.


# P&O TANKSHIPS LTD.

## SHIPS MANAGED ON BEHALF OF OTHER OWNERS

**PM1.  IRISHGATE**          1993-1994

Cf. P&O Tankships  Ltd. Owned Ships No. P15.

**PM2.  NORTHGATE**          1993-1994

Cf. P&O Tankships Ltd. Owned Ships No. P16.

**PM3.  ANCHORMAN (II)**          1993-1996

Cf. Rowbotham. Owned Ships No. 53.

**PM4.  CHARTSMAN (III)**          1993-1996

Cf. Rowbotham. Owned Ships No. 54.

**PM5.  RUDDERMAN (III)**          1994-1996

Cf. Rowbotham. Owned Ships No. 55.

**PM6.  STEERSMAN (V)**          1994-1996

Cf. Rowbotham. Owned Ships No. 56.

# INDEX

| | | | | | | |
|---|---|---|---|---|---|---|
| ORIONMAN | 38 | 62 | X-CLASS LIGHTERS | M1 | 89 |
| OSCO INGRAM OSPREY | R2 | 114 | Y-22 | M40 | 103 |
| OSCO TAMPIMEX EAGLE | R9 | 118 | Y-23 | M41 | 103 |
| PER | R4 | 115 | Y-31 | M49 | 105 |
| POINTSMAN (I) | 22 | 50 | Y-32 | M50 | 105 |
| POINTSMAN (II) | 31 | 57 | Y-40 | M51 | 106 |
| POLARISMAN | 37 | 61 | Y-78 | M52 | 106 |
| PRINCESS | 1 | 36 | Y-82 | M53 | 107 |
| | | | Y-83 | M54 | 107 |
| QUARTERMAN (I) | 21 | 49 | Y-104 | M55 | 107 |
| QUARTERMAN (II) | 36 | 60 | | | |
| QUARTERMAN (III) | P17 | 79 | | | |
| | | | | | |
| RECTOR | M5 | 90 | | | |
| RUDDERMAN (I) | 13 | 43 | | | |
| RUDDERMAN (II) | 30 | 56 | | | |
| RUDDERMAN (III) | 55 | 74 | | | |
| | | | | | |
| SABINE | M15 | 94 | | | |
| SAINT TUDNO | M7 | 91 | | | |
| SALT CREEK | M33 | 100 | | | |
| SALVONIA | M13 | 93 | | | |
| SAXET | M36 | 101 | | | |
| SEA GIANT | M16 | 94 | | | |
| ST. TEATH | M10 | 92 | | | |
| ST. TUDY | M11 | 92 | | | |
| STEERSMAN (I) | 8 | 39 | | | |
| STEERSMAN (II) | 11 | 40 | | | |
| STEERSMAN (III) | 15 | 44 | | | |
| STEERSMAN (IV) | 32 | 57 | | | |
| STEERSMAN (V) | 56 | 75 | | | |
| STELLAMAN (I) | 40 | 64 | | | |
| STELLAMAN (II) | P14 | 77 | | | |
| STEN | R6 | 116 | | | |
| SULPHUR BLUFF | M37 | 102 | | | |
| | | | | | |
| TANKERMAN | 50 | 70 | | | |
| TILLERMAN (I) | 12 | 42 | | | |
| TILLERMAN (II) | 25 | 52 | | | |
| TILLERMAN (III) | 52 | 72 | | | |
| TONKAWA | M34 | 101 | | | |
| | | | | | |
| VEGAMAN | 41 | 64 | | | |
| | | | | | |
| WESTGATE | 49 | 70 | | | |
| WHEELSMAN (I) | 9 | 40 | | | |
| WHEELSMAN (II) | 14 | 43 | | | |
| WHEELSMAN (III) | 28 | 54 | | | |
| WHEELSMAN (IV) | P18 | 80 | | | |